THE NECESSITY OF THE IMPOSSIBLE

Philosophy's Quest for Radical Change

by

Nicole des Bouvrie

Exilic Press,

First edition.
Published in the Netherlands by Exilic Press, 2019.

This work was originally presented as a PhD thesis at
the European Graduate School (supervisor: Dr. Anne Dufourmantelle)
and awarded a summa cum laude after the defense on August 12th, 2017
in Saas Fee, Switzerland, for the defense committee consisting of
Dr. Anne Dufourmantelle, Dr. Avital Ronell and Dr. Laurence Rickels.

Cover design by Nicole des Bouvrie.

ISBN: 9789083016405 (paperback)

www.exilicpress.com

"...what in me is dark illumine,
what is low raise and support..."
~ John Milton, *Paradise Lost*

for my mother

prologue

By choosing to write about the desire to reach the impossible and the closely related illusion of change, I have chosen to fail. To fail in life. To fail in thinking.

As a person, even as a philosopher, one is supposed to be part of the *grande* illusion of radicality, of the idea of revolutionary change that keeps the world in its clutches, that keeps it moving, that keeps complete nihilism and relativism at bay for as long as possible. Change as such is a necessary illusion that keeps human beings sane. It creates the idea of control and belonging. And by trying to undo this mask, behind which there is not truth but merely another mask, as Deleuze already warned us, or even by trying to merely point at it, there are only two options left: either one goes insane, as did Nietzsche when he realised the necessity to re-valuate everything from the ground up, or one dies knowing to have fundamentally failed. At least, this is what one is made to believe when studying philosophy in a world that measures value economically.

What to do when faced with this choice, failing or going mad? One can try to run away from insanity and failure by becoming a politician, a critic, a commentator or even a novelist. In other words, one can choose to cloud the reality that one is doomed to find when one scratches the surface of the paradigms humanity has so masterfully created to remain content with their lives. But then one loses the right to call oneself a philosopher.

Because of the inner calling to reach for a 'new' that is unrelated to the present, to reach for that which lies beyond the realm of the possible, I started out on this path. And I will continue to do so, to search for some form of truth while facing the evidence that truth does not exist. To search for meaning in a meaningless world. To search for change in a world that values only eternal repetition.

This search that will fail to give a definite answer is not only the only thing left. It is also the beginning of all that is human.

A note on the text:

For all quotes in languages other than English, the translation is paraphrased in the text itself. All translations are by the author, unless otherwise specified. All references are put in a footnote so as not to interrupt the flow of the text. For the sake of clarity all pronouns are used in its female form, so that referring to myself, man and mankind is beyond distinction.

A note on this edition:

Writing is a going through iterations of the same. And looking back is to show the difference that comes to light, that relationship to a past self that is destroyed through its desire to be seen.

It's been several years since I first started thinking this project, and a couple of years since I defended it in front of my PhD-committee at the European Graduate School, consisting of Anne Dufourmantelle (my supervisor, who risked her life in more than one sense), Avital Ronell and Laurence Rickels. Much has changed for me since, but I've stayed true to Anne's words whispered after that indefensible defence... that it was good, that I shouldn't change anything.

So this book is loyal to the subject I once was, and in it one can find the traces, the roots of the research I've done since. I would like to thank the time given to me to continue this research by Marie Harder at Fudan University, Shanghai, China, and Hoda Mahmoudi at University of Maryland, United States.

And I'd also like to thank the people who have seen this work growing during the years, and who managed to stand by it, and me. They'll know who they are.

introduction

"[Philosophy's] purpose is never to discuss any philosophical theses, since to do so it would have to share its norms."
~ Alain Badiou, *Wittgenstein's Antiphilosophy*

TASK OF THE PHILOSOPHER

There is only philosophy. There is nothing but the world. Whatever can be considered real and true, or unreal and false, can only exist because of and within philosophy. We always *already* conceive of this word, this page, this place, this truth. We are always *already* present, thinking and reflecting. The world is always already present. Why then is there a need for philosophy?

When philosophy focuses on what *is* – what is present, what is real, what is known – it gets trapped in structuralism: it gets trapped into the idea that there is only structure, that thought and life is all within structure and that there is no escape. But, there is more, there is that which escapes the structure of the present, namely the beyond – the impossible, that which cannot be framed. When one abandons the quest for the impossible, that what is not and may never be, there is nothing beyond that which already is. Philosophy trapped in the present structure would be no more than the piling of words that formulate theories to give yet another view on things; Theories as a description of human behaviour; Theories as an excuse for a specific kind of behaviour; Theories which at most open an unexplored field of meaning of what already is. The problem with this kind of theoretical philosophy is that its vision is always and necessarily limited to its own domain. The theory of gravity will not explain to us why gravity is, what reality there is to it, and what makes us perceive and understand the world according to that specific structure. And as there is only the present in which the law of gravity is the lens through which we perceive the world around us, we are already trapped in a world which is structured around and by it. The theory and the accompanying scientific descriptions and explications enunciate this reality for us. It is not to say that these kinds of theories cannot be used. In certain respects, they have proven to be very useful. But these theories have also caused problems, and if philosophy is to contribute to a new understanding that brings new solutions, it needs to be able to step outside of the limits imposed upon itself through the reality of the present. Therefore, it is left up to the other, to the one who finds herself outside of that reality, to decide upon how and when to apply the present theories.

Were philosophy reduced to descriptive theory, it would become a non-committal set of explanations.[1] It could be abused to fit any type of behaviour. Descriptive philosophers become puppets of contemporary trends, trapped within the ideology that their thinking can only repeat. It is no surprise that faced with contemporary nihilism and structuralism, scientific philosophers become pure relativists and dismiss any claim regarding truth, and refute anything that goes beyond materialism. They are forced to conclude that there is only what is. *Es gibt, was es gibt.* This results in a reality in which the originality as that what lies outside of what is already the case, becomes and remains impossible.

Philosophy might also concern itself with systems, with theories, with structures of thought. This type of philosophy could be compared to other sciences, in that it creates models of reality based on empirical data received from this reality. Social sciences for instance, perceive a phenomenon and try to understand this phenomenon by first creating a descriptive and successively an explanatory model. It is within this circle of producing models of understanding that they continue to operate, and not without merit. However, the underlying assumptions are almost always left untouched. Mathematical models are created to simulate human behaviour and intend to be a model that is as close to reality as possible. The assumptions used to create such a model are, however, not simple facts, but specific choices based on a present understanding of reality. These choices are often considered redundant and are not made

1 See also Friedrich Nietzsche, *Beyond Good and Evil*, section 14, p.45.

explicit. There is a necessity in the prevalence of the present, so any alternative doesn't need to be considered. But even a perfect model of reality cannot account for something that is in no way related to the present: the beyond, that which is not included in the present state of being, that what I name 'the impossible'.

Therefore, in a world in which science works with models of reality that consider only the present reality and how we understand it, there is an enormous task for philosophy. Philosophy is necessary to question how and why the general structure of thought is in place. This is more than a moral statement. The question as to whether or not philosophy might have some moral duty within society is not under consideration here. It is important to notice that philosophy is to concern itself with notions, concepts, understanding, with thoughts and words, not with actual facts in the sense of empirical knowledge. This might form the basis of the misconception that science is considered to contribute something to society and human understanding, whereas philosophy supposedly lingers on in the dark, useless, poetic corridors of life. Social science increases our understanding of present social patterns of behaviour to anticipate the future better. Philosophy does no such thing, it does not concern itself with analysing the present. At least, it shouldn't. Instead, philosophy must be aware of all the structures present, and then refrain from accepting them, from falling asleep. To stay with Nietzsche, the philosopher's task "*is wakefulness itself*".[2]

The problem that contemporary philosophy faces regarding the general passiveness that controls most of the population, philosophers included, can be compared with the tendency of calling photographs 'beautiful'. Although there is nothing wrong with 'beauty' *an sich*, there is a tendency to look at a photograph, decide whether it is beautiful or not, and to move on. However, the real power of photography lies in the fact that it moves you. Or that it

2 Friedrich Nietzsche, *Preface to Beyond Good and Evil*, p.32.

does not. Labelling a photograph beautiful is therefore an insult; it limits the phenomenon to an aesthetic category. A photograph can be boring, superficial, blunt, irritating, etc. But at least it creates a response in the experience of the observer, which is what a photograph (or art in general) is meant to do. The same is true for philosophy. When the only response from society when somehow getting in touch with a certain philosophy is that it is 'great' or 'radical' or whatever, it misses the point. Anything that can even be considered philosophy needs to create a tension in the person involved in it. It is not to give answers, it shouldn't even create yet another paradigm, another manner in which to relate to reality, the world or even a specific phenomenon. Instead, it should occupy the thoughts of the individual and linger on afterwards as an invitation to think.[3]

Unfortunately, there are always examples of thinkers who profess to philosophise whereas they are merely describing reality, grounding an opinion on matters by referencing older thinkers or by commenting on phenomena from a meta-perspective. They apply thought to experience, to prevent, to sustain, to push along or influence the status quo of present power structures. They follow the idea that thought is the conditioning, the limiting, through which that which is possible is delineated. Or, as Herbert Spencer already wrote in 1862, and which continues to be a statement showing the unawareness of the possibilities inherent in the project of philosophy, they say that "[t]o think is to condition; and conditional limitation is the fundamental law of the possibility of thought. For, as the greyhound cannot outstrip his shadow, nor (by a more appropriate simile) the eagle outsoar the atmosphere in which he floats, and by which alone he may be supported; so the mind cannot transcend that sphere of limitation, within and through which exclusively the possibility of thought is realized."[4]

3 See: Martin Heidegger, *What is Called Thinking?*
4 Herbert Spencer, *First Principles*, p.75.

This is not what philosophy is. Reality is not its limit, as it is for science. Yes, philosophy can be considered a means to delineate the contemporary discourse and to indicate the limits, consequences and underlying structure of this prevalent understanding of what is. But at the same time, philosophy needs to be a putting between brackets of what is normally considered truth and reality, in order to wonder about its existence. It is easy to see how some would label this approach to philosophy naive and superfluous. People often wonder why we should examine reality in a non-empirical way. And that critique is valid, as one of the dangers of philosophy as such, and of this kind of non-empirical approach in general, would be that such an account of contemporary thought and understanding never leaves the historical domain. As a purely historical overview philosophy would be of limited value to contemporary life.

Therefore, it is good to reassert that philosophy is not meant to limit itself to being a critique of history, of modernity, of the present. Instead, philosophy is to be understood as a method to trace the underlying structures of thought in order to get a better understanding of the whole. This is what I will do in Chapter 1. But we need to be careful to make sure we do not do this to merely re-confirm these structures and to gloat in our present understanding of reality. Instead, the goal of philosophy, the reason why it might start out with the delineation of the limits and possibilities of the present world, as I will do in part 1, is to make way for the possibilities of breaking the present in which we find ourselves. This motive already influences the way we will trace the foundation upon which reality is structured. From the first moment, the nature of reality is approached, this ulterior motive influences our every move. Because in the end, it is not continuation of an everlasting stream of consciousness that is the theme here. "To criticize a time like our rotten present, is easy and is uninteresting, when it doesn't provide a way out."[5] It is not critique *an sich* that is our concern, but the finding of a 'solution', of a way out of the problematic structure we find ourselves in, which constructs both the society around us and our own thinking. Philosophy's goal is to search for a way out of this present. It is to search for a way in which an alternative present, when approached, can be recognized and taken on. It is precisely in the breaking of this present, in describing and envisioning this in specific and unclouded terms that is the goal of this book, which will be proposed in the third part. It is the radical change that un-relates to the world that is, that beckons the new that was hitherto unimagined, yes even impossible.

Searching for this impossible, we follow in the footsteps of Wittgenstein: we need to observe what cannot be talked about, namely the beyond. The impossible. The infinite. We need to acknowledge we cannot talk about it, and then continue to voice it, question it, talk about it, speak about it. Much is at stake.

This is not an academic exercise. This is not a moral statement based on some pre-framed ideology. In fact, if we need to trace where this desire for the impossible comes from, and indeed we must, for the desire creates the way we understand this longing, we need to point at our being human. The world is given, everything is already there. But if we remain silent about that which is not, in the face of the other that is our immediate desire, we are left alone, destitute even of our own self. Without our reaching for the impossible, we can never become human. Or can we? Once we realise this longing of the human becoming, the necessity of reaching for the impossible, the beyond, we will realise that there is nothing else one *can* talk about. This paradoxical state, where the philosopher realizes she is what limits the understanding of reality, and the possible madness that follows when the breaking of this structure is taken serious, is what will be discussed in part II.

5 Wolfgang Schirmacher, *Technik und Gelassenheit,* p.9.

Philosophy "must set limits to what can be thought; and, in doing so, to what cannot be thought."[6] Fortunately for us, philosophy does not have to put these limits in place, they only need to be uncovered. The world is always already there, claiming us, framing us, limiting us from the moment of our coming-into-being. Therefore, we cannot follow in the footsteps of Wittgenstein, and it must become clear that his claim that philosophy will be able to "signify what cannot be said, by presenting clearly what can be said"[7] is an illusion. That what lies beyond can never be obtained by modelling the present.

Yet by questioning that what lies beyond the limits of our thinking, we enter a dangerous paradox. We are at once acknowledging and dismissing structuralism. "If all thought is limitation; —if whatever we conceive is, by the very act of conception, regarded as finite, —the infinite, from a human point of view, is merely a name for the absence of those conditions under which thought is possible. To speak of a *Conception of the Infinite* is, therefore, at once to affirm those conditions and to deny them."[8]

Oh, how wonderful it would be, if we could return to the time before we tried to become masters over the world. Before the tower of Babel was constructed, we would speak each other's language, but more importantly, every word would be the truth itself, not this dim reflection of the image of what is. We would be able to speak and create at the same time. Why did we humans try to master it all, why did we not understand that the world is already forcing us to think, and why was our ultimate punishment the creation of distinct languages, with each translation, with each uttering of a distinctiveness, moving us further away from that which we considered once to be clear and truthful? Oh, why should I be aware of all this, speaking multiple languages, but unable to use them depending on whatever is more true to the moment, why can't I talk about verstehen *and am I left with the word* comprehension *instead?*

6 Ludwig Wittgenstein, *Tractatus logico-philosophicus*, §4.114.
7 Ludwig Wittgenstein, *Tractatus logico-philosophicus*, §4.115.
8 Herbert Spencer, *First Principles*, p.77.

QUEST FOR THE IMPOSSIBLE

Philosophy is the quest to think the impossible. It is up to science to describe what is possible, what is present and knowable. The history of science confirms this: whenever a philosopher became more concerned with the empirical present instead of the impossible, which is not included in the present and which lies beyond language and the knowable, a new science was born.[9] It is therefore inconceivable that those who profess to be philosophers merge themselves with being scientists, or with opinions and other statistical data, as they belong solely to the present.

Facing the impossible, acknowledging the groundlessness of contemporary (Western) society and thought, searching for something that lies outside the realm of truth and sanity, a philosopher fights until death. She will be the last woman standing when the last wave of nihilism and relativism makes even the quest for failure seem not worthy of existence, of being thought.

This search for the impossible is in no way what Alain Badiou has referred to as a pleading guilty of philosophy in his first *Manifesto for Philosophy*. It is in no way saying "in fact that philosophy is impossible, completed, assigned to something other than itself."[10] When Jean-François Lyotard proclaimed that "[p]hilosophy as architecture has been ruined,"[11] this in no way hails the end of philosophy. It should be considered as precisely the opposite, something Badiou realised in his second manifesto several years later, in which he mentions that philosophy is to be "dedicated to its revolutionary pertinence (against the servile dogmatism making it a component of Western propaganda)."[12]

9 Thanks to professor Albert van Helden, personal conversations, 2006.
10 Alain Badiou, *Manifesto for Philosophy*, p.27.
11 As quoted by Alain Badiou, *Manifesto for Philosophy*, p.28.
12 Alain Badiou, *Second Manifesto for Philosophy*, p.119.

But why is it that we fight the groundlessness that is the present? Why do philosophers take it upon themselves to continue thinking the impossible, facing failure, fully aware that the powerful structures that surround us are the results of a dogmatic attitude, as can for instance be found in the philosophy of the academy? We need to look back to advance, and we are confronted with Meno's paradox. We are still facing this very same paradox, of questioning the beyond, whereas we're actually questioning ourselves:

> Meno: And how will you search for something, when you don't know what it is at all? I mean, which of the things you don't know will you take in advance and search for, when you don't know what it is? Or even if you come right up against it, how will you know that it's the unknown thing you're looking for?
>
> Socrates: I see what you're getting at, Meno. Do you realize what a controversy you're conjuring up? The claim is that it's impossible for a man to search either for what he knows or for what he doesn't know: he wouldn't be searching for what he knows, since he knows it and that makes the search unnecessary, and he can't search for what he doesn't know either, since he doesn't even know what it is he's going to search for.[13]

In response to this paradox Plato answers that it makes us better people when we continue to think, in which thinking implies that we are concerned with questions we believe we have no chance of finding answers for. But this is not a logical argument. Why would we face the impossible to be 'better people'? It makes no sense if this is a manner to put oneself above others to find a reason for existence. Plato's argument as a judgement should be avoided, as it lies in the contemporary.

13 Plato, *Meno*, §80d-e.

We should always try to go beyond judgement, before judgement – to the paradise in which names and truth are still equivalents.[14] Where language is not judgement, but truth-telling. Where, as before Babel's fiasco, language is reality, instead of merely reflecting to a structure of images.

Plato's insightful response to the paradox of the impossibility to think beyond the limits of our knowing, does link the impossible to something which we could describe by being human. Searching for the impossible, the quest of philosophy, is not merely a theoretical exercise, there is something at stake. It is not a moral judgment, but our human becoming that is dependent upon our reaching for the impossible.

14 See Walter Benjamin's notion on revelation in his essay "On Language as Such and the Language of Man" in: *Reflections*.

THINKING THE IMPOSSIBLE

That philosophy concerns itself with thinking the impossible, or at least that it should concern itself with thinking the impossible, is not a novel thought. Yet despite the work of so many philosophers, philosophy is still often only used to confirm the present order of things. This is what is nowadays, following Plato, referred to as sophism. It is not a problem to be a lover of wisdom, but, as is often the case when it concerns love, to love is also to be blinded by the object of your love. To call oneself a philosopher, it is necessary to continue to question one's truth, even when the consequences of doing so are grave. Yet at the same time we are obliged to notice what it means, to identify a necessity, what happens when one describes a desire that forces us into a certain direction. Even this pointing to a necessity, a need, something one should, is already problematic. It limits, it frames, it directs. It is not surprising that so many great thinkers from Western history have an 'early' and a 'late' version of their work. For any discovery that might at one moment seem to leap, to rupture the present, is then subsumed in the framework of reality, and will later on need to be escaped all over again. Therefore, one who portrays himself to be in possession of truth, is to be considered with caution when one is interested in truth. This warning belongs to the foundation of the Western philosophical tradition, which has occupied itself with moving away from sophism since the beginning of thinking and writing. And although this is common knowledge and has been for such a long time, the threat of sophism is still very much present today.

Alain Badiou warns us against the tendency of philosophy as a means to propagate the dominant values of the social order we have to endure.[15] Yet it is not easy to do this, when one is faced with the world and is confronted with the necessity of taking one's place in

15 See: Alain Badiou, *Ethics*.

that very same world. Perhaps, the Derridian 'perhaps', we even must come to the conclusion that Badiou himself fails to do this. Because it is not enough to state that one distances herself from thoughts that belong to the contemporary discourses, one must step out of its influence altogether. In the case of Badiou we can easily detect a longing for a type of humanism and progress that is not founded outside our present discourses. Although Badiou is describing and formalising situations and events, he is himself, in describing these, not independent of the world he inhabits. Some might say it is inevitable to succumb to the world you live in. Yet this is philosophy's task, to discover whether this succumbing is inevitable. Philosophy thus embodies the desire of the stepping out of the world and to risk one's sanity, to chase fundamental, radical change – even when or even precisely because it turns out to be impossible.

Chasing the impossible, questioning the structure taken for granted, breaking the epistemic reality that is always already present, longing for radical change – this is the task I have set myself. But it is also a task that has been set for me, as it is inherent in the assignment of being human. And as such, it is not something *I* do, it is a shared enterprise. It is only because of the other that mirrors me, that questions my every moment of existence, that this being human, this quest for the impossible is ever addressed.

But in chasing this question, by writing this, by putting it into language, by taking my place in the world, answering a question which forces me to concern myself with the foundation of worldly affairs, philosophy faces another paradox. When philosophers do not speak, when they do not communicate, they are lost in this age in which it seems that the right type of marketing is the only way to be heard. Yet it is a fundamental problem when philosophy is preoccupied with commercialising itself in order to be understood. This is what Lyotard warned us for: "The same goes for writers and thinkers: if they resist the predominant use of time today, they are not only predestined to disappear, but they must also contribute to the making of a 'sanitary cordon' isolating themselves. In the shelter of this cordon, their destruction is supposed to be able to be put off for a while. But they 'buy' this brief and vain delay by modifying their way of thinking and writing in such a way that their works become more or less communicable, exchangeable; in a word, commercializable."[16]

Language itself is already such 'commerce'. By using language in such a way that it can be understood by others, one already bends one's thought to the structures present in society. Even before that, before communicating it to the other, am I not always already thinking in words and structures? The problem of structuralism, of thinking that everything is dependent on the structures of thought and the frames of language, lies also in the fact that I have been continuously trained and educated to follow the existing structures and languages to function 'properly' in the structure we call society. Even reality itself and everything that is possible is no more than a specific structure that is shared. But can I allow for this structure to make up the or my whole world?

Even if I can take up arms against this, if I truly want to stand up against this 'system', I will need to think of places in which such rebellion is allowed, or at least can take shape, is somehow possible. Not only is this true for social groups protesting in the streets, who need to get a permit that allows them to legally demonstrate during a specific time and in a specific place. It is also true inside of our own structures of thought. There is no escape. But succumbing and following the rules of the structure of thought, to leave aside my human desire for the impossible, is out of the question. But all the acceptable and accessible manners in which I can protest the system, still leave me inside the 'system', make me even a necessary part of the system. Even 'being against' something limits one to be part of the very structure one opposes. Whether you say yes or no, the question

16 François Lyotard, *The Inhuman*, p.76.

remains the same. It is like looking into a mirror. It is you who looks, and you see yourself. Even though everything is reversed, mirrored, left has become right, it is still you. The mirror itself structures, it literally frames what you see.

This is what Wittgenstein understood very well. For something to be possible is unrelated to whether something exists or not. Agitating against something, negating its existence is one of the core responses within a structure, it is a grounding of the very structure that creates and sustains the possibility of this 'something'. Therefore, philosophy should go beyond any positioning, which posits reality in a specific place and time. It should undo itself of the influence of any system or structure that is limiting what is possible.

Philosophy should thus distance itself from any totalitarianism. Following the discourses present in society, presenting oneself in a manner that is acceptable and tolerated or doing precisely that by doing the exact opposite, is already giving in to totalitarianism – whether one calls it society, truth or reality. This is a paradox that presents everyone who is interested in original thinking with a difficulty that is not easily overcome. Whatever is done, the moment a thought is captured in any language that is communicable to others and to ourselves, the thinking changes and is grounded in the present. Any original thinking that might occur is altered in such a way to confirm the basic assumptions and notions that communication deals with. Which is why we should heed Heidegger's call to always think everything again. Over and over again.

For us there is only one thing left, as Wolfgang Schirmacher put it so adequately: "The only thing left for us is to withstand the ordinary, which presents itself continually as a 'new path'."[17] We must withstand the normalcy that presents itself as continual variations of the 'new way'. But we will need to acknowledge our limits, and

17 Wolfgang Schirmacher, *Technik und Gelassenheit,* p.9.

continue to strive towards originality, whatever the consequences. Not another mere variation, a continuation of what has always already been present. No, what we need to strive towards is a break, a rupture. A fundamental change. This is philosophy's quest for the impossible.

The task of the philosopher is thus different from giving an overview of what other philosophers have said. Although this is what our present educational system tries to sell us, that the repeating of ideas is good enough, this is one of the ways in which original thinking is pushed out, is crushed under the power of examples, under the authority of (the thoughts of) others. But at the same time, these thoughts do matter, because they frame how we think about the matter. And, to be honest, how can we teach children or ourselves original thinking? Were it not for us, they would all be thinking creatively. Knowledge frames creativity, it destroys that what made it creativity in the first place. Or does creativity also rely on the structures present, as it releases itself by breaking that what frames it in the first place?

Despite all the resistance present in society, we all continue to long for it, this essential rupture, this fundamental change that leaves us only with the beyond, the impossible.

27

PART I

Before we start trying to formulate or even answer any questions, let us first consider the terminology that is in use, to situate the frame, to frame the frame in relation to everything that already is. Framing the frame is like tracing the architecture of thought, setting up the space that separates that what is from that what is not.

INTRODUCTION

> "Philosophy opposes the unity and universality of truth to the plurality and relativity of opinions."
> ~ Alain Badiou, *Philosophy for Militants*

Philosophy should busy itself with thinking that which is not, that which lies beyond, with the impossible. To approach the impossible, the beyond, we first need to find out what is, *was es gibt*. How to think this, what vocabulary to use and how to delineate this is not obvious, as it is hidden beyond the everydayness of things which obstructs to see it clearly. Even situating the what-is is already problematic, as it raises questions that place this thinking in the realm of metaphysics and epistemology. Framing the frame through which to discuss the impossible is however a necessary step in order to limit ourselves before breaking free of it, so these issues will need to be addressed before moving on to tracing a constructive answer to the question regarding the impossible. Acknowledging the longing for the impossible, for the change that reaches beyond that what is, and acknowledging that this change is always related to that which is, there is no other place to start this discussion except in the present, in reality itself.

Reality is only situated in the present. There is only the moment in which we are, which includes a relation to past and future. As Immanuel Kant already showed us, it is the synthesis of the manifold, the fundamental activity of the human mind, the human ability to put different representations together and grasping them into one (act of) knowledge,[18] which creates a unity of understanding. The ability to perceive anything as a whole, is a human capability. Origin, future, colour, consequence – all are human constructions. We could even argue these are not merely human, but actually social construc-

18 Immanuel Kant, *Kritik der reinen Vernunft*, A77/B103.

tions. In other words, our observations and understanding is not to be taken as objective reality. It is the human synthesis that is "the whole of conscious life".[19] We, human beings, decide what we see, what we feel, what we do, what we hear. And perhaps more importantly, we decide what it means.

Although the human experience is thus coloured and situated in the *human* understanding of everything, this does not mean that reality is limited by this relation, or created by it, as some idealists might say. Saying anything beyond the *human* perception of reality is pointless, without making everything anyone can utter merely subjective. But this perception of reality, and our understanding of reality will always be subjective as it is foremost *human*.

But what about language? There is some truth in the parable of *Genesis*, in which the world was created according to the word, and the word and the world were the same. Whereas words are often only representations of the world, or vice versa (this is beyond our knowledge), Walter Benjamin points us in the direction of the creative power of the word as naming.[20] Language after Eden is always a judging, a referencing to something else, a comparison, a relating to something that is beyond our grasp. Whereas in original language, the language of creation, the original word is precisely that 'what is'.

As such, it seems that language, in its original sense of language at the time of creation, can provide an important insight when we are interested in 'what is'. Words did not appear, they were forged in the same fire as reality itself. Words were commensurate with the world. But what happened? According to Benjamin, the translation of the language of things into human language is not just the translation of the voiceless into sound, but the translation of the nameless

19 Edmund Husserl, *Cartesian Meditations: An Introduction to Pure Phenomenology*, p.42.
20 See Walter Benjamin, "On Language as Such and on the Language of Man", In: *Gesammelte Schriften II.*

into a name.[21] The name, the language, does not have meaning of itself, but communicates the spirit of the thing.[22] This would mean that there is this original truth inside the original words, the words that belong to the things themselves. Would it then be enough to trace the etymology of the world back to their original meaning, to find out what is real?

This tracing could be seen as an utmost Platonic movement, a moving beyond the shadows of the cave and into the light, into the world of Ideals, the truth. By reaching this world of truth that lies hidden within or beyond the everydayness of experience, do we reach that 'what is'? Is it still human *being* that we are then talking about, or does the Platonic movement take us to an original state that we can in no way relate to anymore?

According to the early Heidegger, the most important question is the question of 'being', the question of that 'what is.' Not just because the answer is lacking, but because the question itself is dark and without direction.[23] Human being, the human consciousness, is however always already linked to the present by way of being, as it is thrown into it. There is no human being beyond or before this connectedness to the present. Human being is therefore always already linked to the given present, the world. The ontological character of being (*Dasein*) is not a Platonic Idea nor a Kantian *cogito* according to Heidegger, but needs to take place, a specific place (*da*), by finding a possibility, an opening in reality: *Da-sein*.[24]

21 Walter Benjamin, *Gesammelte Schriften II*, p.151.
22 Walter Banjamin, *Gesammelte Schriften II*, p.142.
23 Martin Heidegger, *Sein und Zeit*, p.6.
24 Martin Heidegger, *Sein und Zeit*, p.43.

The later Heidegger also acknowledges the link to language. Being is from then on placed within the realm of language, language becomes the 'House of Being'.[25] Yet this does not resolve our desire for the impossible. In fact, it merely places us, frames us, puts us in a specific spot (*Ge-stell*).

Tracing the idea of what can be known as a philosophical historical overview does not help us to get to an understanding of the impossible. Whatever philosophical position we take, this position is a contemporary and therefore a temporary one. The problem is, even when it is clear what the limits of the present frame are, that it is hard and perhaps even impossible to look beyond this frame of thought. Once you're inside it, everything that is and can be, all possibilities and impossibilities, are part of this frame. There is no creation that goes beyond it, it is the frame itself that creates all possibilities. Once we find ourselves in a position, a place in relation to what lies outside of it, we are framed: There is no beyond, there are no limits that can be crossed. This is true of all comprehensive systems of thought, even ones that try to account for that what is not included, the beyond. One could even say that trying to impose a system of thought that enforces the beyond is in itself nothing less than tyranny: it not only allows for the 'what is', but also frames and limits that beyond.

25 Martin Heidegger, *Letter on Humanism*, p. 217.

THE FRAME

> "What is, doesn't *become*; what is becoming, *is* not. Now they all believe, even with doubt, in that what is."
> ~ Friedrich Nietzsche, *Götzen-Dämmerung*

To trace the frame, let us look at several notions as they are introduced by a variety of thinkers. Each term can at first be approached as a separate entity, and its perspective on change and the impossible must be carefully considered. Finally, however, our goal here is a comprehensive understanding of the frame, overcoming the terminology and moving towards a workable definition of 'what is.'

To do so, we need to keep in mind that everything is always embedded in the world. This is true for whatever definition of 'world' we use, whether we focus on the ontological nature of beings, following Badiou who describes world as an ontologically-closed set, or whether we look at Heidegger who distinguished between the *ontological* and the *ontic* world.

To determine what this *world* consists of and how it is structured, we inevitably think alongside several philosophers who have contributed towards our understanding of this concept. By tracing different theories, we should not only create a better working understanding that will help us to position the concept of the impossible and the possibility of change, but also differentiate between the many philosophical conceptions – such as *episteme*, *paradigm*, *Weltanschauung* etc. – that have been voiced in order to talk about this *world*.

ON THE EPISTEME

An *episteme* is a system which shapes the body of knowledge and perspectives that are present at a certain moment and place in time and space. The *episteme* is a common ground, "the total set of relations that unite, at a given period, the discursive practices that give rise to epistemological figures, sciences, and possibly formalized systems."[26] "The episteme is not a form of knowledge (*connaissance*) or type of rationality which, crossing the boundaries of the most varied sciences, manifests the sovereign unity of a subject, a spirit, or a period; it is the totality of relations that can be discovered, for a given period, between the sciences when one analyses them at the level of discursive regularities."[27] The episteme is always contemporaneous. In other words, it is limited and structured in a specific time.

The episteme is not the content of the discourses present, but the underlying networks and frames which bring these discourses about. So how then can we find out the epistemic reality of something, how can we find out what a specific episteme looks like? Foucault calls exploring the episteme a type of 'archaeology'. Deleuze and Guattari refer to this when they talk about 'a map'.[28] The episteme is a structure whose elements themselves they do not signify.[29]

In his book *The Order of Things* (*Les Mots et les choses,* 1966), Foucault explores whether there exists a "certain code of knowledge,"[30] a system beyond the empirical notions that fill these systems with facts and understandings. He describes "a network of analogies that transcended the traditional proximities"[31] between the different areas that he examines (biology, linguistics, economy). He outlines what

26 Michel Foucault, *Archaeology of Knowledge*, p.211.
27 Michel Foucault, *Archaeology of Knowledge*, p.211.
28 See: Gilles Deleuze and Félix Guattari, *A Thousand Plateaus.*
29 See: Jacques Derrida, *Marges de la philosophie*, p.161-62.
30 Michel Foucault, *The Order of Things*, p.x.
31 Michel Foucault, *The Order of Things*, p.xi.

he calls 'an epistemological space'. By positively outlining this unconscious space – that which influences people involved in a specific (scientific) discourse in a specific time and in a specific place – Foucault shows how underlying unconscious "rules of formation" produce the concepts and theories present in the discourse. The episteme itself has neither external signs, nor inner meaning.[32]

Foucault referred to this uncovering of the underlying epistemological space as archaeological. This should not be conceived as archaeological in a historical sense, although Foucault did survey histories. His archaeology is not a history of ideas, which would entail a describing of knowledge that serves as "an empirical, unreflective basis for subsequent formalizations."[33] "[A]rchaeological description is precisely such an abandonment of the history of ideas, a systematic rejection of its postulates and procedures, an attempt to practise a quite different history of what men have said."[34] Instead of finding out *what* has been said, we need to understand what has been *said*. We need to move beyond the symbols, and move into the sphere of being. As Spencer already said, "Ultimate religious ideas and ultimate scientific ideas, alike turn out to be merely symbols of the actual, not cognitions of it."[35] And to find out what the epistemic structures are that make the specific content of discourse possible, a new understanding of archaeology is necessary.

Archaeology should be thought of more literally, concerning itself with a digging towards unearthing the foundation of thoughts that we normally find and are working with on a more superficial, a more conscious level. Not in the sense that one wants to find what lies beyond 'what is' or what is said, but in the sense that one wants to fully grasp what makes possible for there to be 'what is', what it is precisely that one can distinguish between this specific thing under

32 Gilles Deleuze, *Woran erkennt man den Strukturalismus?* p.11-15.
33 Michel Foucault, *Archaeology of Knowledge*, p.153.
34 Michel Foucault, *Archaeology of Knowledge*, p.154.
35 Herbert Spencer, *First Principles,* p.68.

scrutiny and the rest.[36] "It is not an interpretative discipline: it does not seek another, better-hidden discourse."[37] It might be that these underlying, proto-, pre-structures that form and define the actual level of what can be present in the conscious body of knowledge, are also existing in a chronological order and could thus be seen as a historical dimension. It would however be a mistake to limit archaeology to being merely a historical account. Instead, archaeology in the Foucaultian sense proposes to differentiate between "the epistemological level of knowledge (or scientific consciousness) and the archaeological level of knowledge."[38] Žižek confirms this, when he enunciates that Foucault "is as far as possible from any form of historicism, of locating events in their historical context-on the contrary, Foucault abstracts them from their reality and its historical causality and studies the immanent rules of their emergence."[39]

Where historical descriptions are considering how something has come about, tracing isolated points, successive ruptures and the continuous line of evolution, an archaeologist of knowledge is interested in approaching the underlying structures that form the foundation for the matter at hand. By doing so, Foucault breaks with what Deleuze calls the Western mind. "It is a regrettable characteristic of the Western mind to relate expressions and actions to the exterior or transcendent ends, instead of evaluating them on a plane of consistency on the basis of their intrinsic value."[40] Approaching the episteme is thus limited to being multiplicities, without beginning or end, "it is always in the middle, between things, interbeing, intermezzo."[41]

36 Michel Foucault, *Archaeology of Knowledge*, p.155.
37 Michel Foucault, *Archaeology of Knowledge*, p.155.
38 Michel Foucault, *The Order of Things*, p.xiv.
39 Slavoj Žižek, *Organs without Bodies*, p.10.
40 Gilles Deleuze and Félix Guattari, *A Thousand Plateaus*, p.22.
41 Gilles Deleuze and Félix Guattari, *A Thousand Plateaus*, p.25.

There is a difficulty when we consider the approach of Foucault, by distinguishing between the epistemological and the archaeological levels of knowledge, and the one propagated by Deleuze and Guattari. Both are interested in valuing the episteme, the plateau of what is, without relating its existence to reproducing "an unconscious closed upon itself, [instead] it constructs the unconscious."[42] Despite the difficulty in attaining this archaeology of the episteme, or the mapping of the plateau, how does this approach deal with the impossible? When accepting the level of the episteme, approaching it, does it encapsulate everything that is? How does an episteme deal with the idea of change, of a search beyond this epistemological space? Foucault acknowledges this problem, saying that "It has been said that this work denies the very possibility of change. And yet my main concern has been with changes."[43] This paradox concerns the phenomenological approach to reality, which ever since Foucault, is still influential today.

Phenomenology's problem with the episteme

When considering Foucault's notion of the episteme and the discourses that are built upon this archaeological reality, it is easy to consider a moving beyond this reality to be impossible, beyond our reach, beyond our possibilities. When our discourse and our outlook upon the world is created, formed by an underlying, unconscious structure, what is left for a human being but to fall into line with the epistemic power that is at play? The notion of human freedom becomes redundant for human existence. Many authors have interpreted Foucault's work in this way, regarding his archaeological project as merely a manner to introduce us to the problem of power in the world. Although I am not discarding Foucault's interest in power structures, there is something greater at play here that should not be overlooked.

42 Gilles Deleuze and Félix Guattari, *A Thousand Plateaus*, p.12.
43 Michel Foucault, *The Order of Things*, p.xii.

The idea that we are locked inside this archaeological reality, in which change becomes impossible to conceive of, is problematic when we hold a phenomenological approach to reality and experience. The phenomenological perspective holds that we as human beings are constantly involved in experiencing the world and reality and have to complete the task of making sense of it, every moment again. The only objective reality is the relation between the subject and the object which the subject is relating to.[44] This results in a need to continuously re-think everything. There is no knowing something itself. As Heidegger has put it: "To experience is in the precise sense of the word: *eundo assequi*: in the going, while underway reaching something, to attain something through the being on a road,"[45] Knowing is thus reduced to *a posteriori* disclosure. The *a priori* field of being is not to be denied: it is unknowable and therefore unimportant to dwell upon. In other words, while the actively tracing, the going, the following the road, the experience itself leads to the disclosure of what is: the underlying reality, the episteme, is thereby reduced to the unconscious and unknowable. Phenomenology thus tries to escape the system, the structure of the episteme.

According to phenomenology, the openness of the human subject to the world that he or she encounters is of the utmost importance. For Heidegger, this openness is related to 'truth' itself, which he refers to as *aletheia,* unconcealedness, openness to what is.[46] Someone may choose or be led to not open herself towards the world, for instance through 'bad faith' (Sartre), but the possibility of openness forms the basis for any claim to being. In a way, being the opposite of open, namely closed to the world, is not really a negative statement, but forms a constitutive moment for each individual. Only because of the closedness, the concealment of being, a greater value is placed on the possibility of openness. We can see this happening in several

44 See for instance Husserl and Brentano.
45 Martin Heidegger, *Unterwegs zur Sprache*, p.169-170.
46 See for instance: Martin Heidegger, *The Origin of the Work of Art*.

places in Heidegger's thinking, for instance when he shows how *das Man* is an essential condition for the being of men and should not to be thought of as a (negative) psychologism, in which *eigentlich sein* is to be preferred over *uneigentlich sein*. It is not authenticity that has to be heralded as the only true way of being – it is rather this connection of the possibility of openness towards the world that founds being. The structure of being is thus explained along the lines of openness-closeness, and the exact content of this relationship is not important in order to understand the episteme in place.

Yet when we take this phenomenological attitude that an individual is able to fully determine her being in the world, the existence of a limiting episteme that Foucault describes is problematic. But on a more basic level both Foucault and Heidegger have a similar outlook on the origin of things. Both Heidegger and Foucault posit that we are always already in the world. This being thrown has however different consequences for each of these thinkers. For Heidegger, this being thrown is the basic existential of our being, something we on the one hand necessarily need to accept, but that we don't need to succumb to, as this being thrown also gives us the possibility of *becoming*. Foucault will agree that our being in the world cannot be denied: we are living within structures that not only were there before we could even notice them, but he shows that this world also structures our thinking, our experience of the world and our attitude towards ourselves and the other. The Foucaultian approach is thus much more focused on the relationship with power, and the limitation of the individual within the power-structure of the episteme. For Heidegger, this power that being has over the individual is not problematised. Whereas for Foucault, this epistemic structure of being is not something stable and beyond change – it is an important concept to investigate and to understand how our experience of reality is dependent upon it. This distinction will be even more important once we try to reach something that lies beyond the episteme.

Beyond the Episteme?

Considering that we set out with the quest for the impossible, lingering on the power the unconscious episteme has over us will bring us no way nearer to our objective. Going beyond powers that cannot be put into words, that cannot be thought, that can only in translation be brought to light, is out of the question. The epistemological space simply *is*, it would be nonsensical to consider a beyond. Anytime we think, see, experience the world, we are already doing that within an epistemic structure, so to ask for a possibility of experience outside of an epistemic structure is simply out of range, makes no sense.

But then, what about change? Whenever Foucault considers a change, this is a change that takes place *within* the epistemological space, without ever leaving it. In his ultimate work on the establishment and changes of the episteme, he never accounts for the reason of change, the moment it takes place or the mechanism of the change itself. Although his analysis is commendable and offers many insights into the development of epistemic structures, and will remain an important work to base much of social science's research on for a long time, his description of a movement from the classical age to the modern understanding of the human sciences is exactly that: a description. It is not a theory, neither does it give ideas which could be projected upon a different movement in history. It is archaeological in an epistemic *and* a historical sense, but it does not provide us with a philosophy of the beyond, the impossible. It does not consider the moment in which any changes were brought to and taken on inside or by the epistemic structure.

More importantly, changes that Foucault describes always takes place within the episteme. A change within the episteme cannot be considered a radical change in which the impossible is reached. There is no break of the possible, the epistemological space remains intact. The elements within the space are re-arranged, possibly ideas are inverted. Therefore, we will call changes within epistemes 'modifications'. Deleuze says these modifications can be likened unto "the furniture we are forever rearranging."[47]

In fact, relying solely on a concept of the episteme when we want to think the impossible, would leave us in existential despair. Probably Foucault understood this himself, and spent the rest of his life approaching different topics and repeating the same archaeological method to uncover changes within the episteme.[48] As if he understood that moving within an epistemological space is like finding oneself trapped within a panopticon of which the limits are internalised and the beyond is out of reach, even non-existent. It is this type of thinking that is at least in part responsible for thinking there is no change, leading to existential despair.

---

47 Gilles Deleuze and Félix Guattari, *A Thousand Plateaus*, p.21.
48 See: Alasdair MacIntyre, *Three Rival Versions of Moral Enquiry*.

Defining the Impossible

The episteme defines the impossible negatively, as it limits that which is possible. The impossible is outside of this limit, and therefore always negatively defined by the episteme. With this I mean that the episteme always shows us what the impossible is not.

When we want to know what the impossible *is*, the episteme does not point us in the right direction. The episteme can only voice that which is *not* in the right direction. It leaves us in a place that cannot be named, a going that is not. Even when considering that which is impossible, we have not left the frame that the episteme has laid down for us.

Derrida referred to this, to his idea about philosophy as a quest for the impossible, as a dwelling on the limits. "I try to keep myself at the limit of philosophical discourse. (…) Thus, the limit on the basis of which philosophy became possible, defined itself as the epistēmē, functioning within a system of fundamental constraints, conceptual oppositions outside of which philosophy becomes impracticable."[49] But although we might point to the impossible as a limit as Derrida does, this does not solve our predicament. The impossible then is still approached from the perspective that is prescribed by the episteme. Let us therefore look to other ways in which to philosophers have constructed the human relation to knowing and thinking.

49 Jacques Derrida, "Implications: Interview with Henri Ronse", in: *Positions*.

DISCOURSE, PARADIGM, WELTANSCHAUUNG, WORLD

Another term important to consider the limits of what can be thought, is the term 'discourse'. 'Discourse' refers to the language-based field of understanding in which a person, a phenomenon or a concept finds itself. It is the conscious translation of the episteme, translating the underlying rules of formation into a knowable realm, specific to its time and place. The term discourse is used nowadays in many different contexts, mostly referring to a specific set of terms and language that is shared among a specific group of people. Judith Butler referred to it as "the limits of acceptable speech."[50]

For Foucault, language is only one type of phenomena that can be examined in order to see the structures of the episteme at work at the level of the discourse. Thus, it is important to not limit our understanding of the term 'discourse' to a linguistic entity. Instead we will take a more general definition and with 'discourse' we will delineate the conscious level of the episteme, focused within a specific sphere where human beings find themselves.

A discourse is a specified arena of truth. Something becomes not only meaningful, but can also contain truth when uttered (*énoncé*) within a discourse. "It is always possible one could speak the truth in a void; one would only be in the true, however, if one obeyed the rules of some discursive 'police' which would have to be reactivated every time one spoke."[51] It is thus the discursive system that allows for judgement between good and evil, in other words the discourse is the level at which 'truth' and truth-procedures come into being. This 'truth' is not to be taken as an objective sort, but only established and valid within the specific discourse to which it belongs.

50 Judith Butler, *Excitable Speech: A Politics of the Performative*. p. 34.
51 Judith Butler, *Excitable Speech: A Politics of the Performative*. p. 34.

Social science has long since picked up on this notion of discourses and the usefulness of analysing these in order to get an understanding of the manner in which discourses are constructed. Take for instance Michael Walzer, who comes to an understanding of power by delineating different discourses on power-structures as being different spheres, each having its own rules and patterns.[52] Some may overlap, but they may rely on their own truth-procedures and as such might be talking about completely different things. A lot of areas in (social) science have been reframed into research on discourse analysis, which makes it possible to describe different spheres of action and attitudes that might overlap or have power over the other.

To understand the relationship between different discourses, discourse analysis analyses semantic occurrences, for instance through counting words or looking at patterns of speech to reveal socio-psychological characteristics of a situation or people. Studying semantic occurrences and descriptive notions can show a status quo of a specific discourse. But what does this mean? When a discourse is limited to a specific moment in time and space, discourse analysis will only be interesting for some political or marketing purpose. Knowing how people speak and which words they use in a specific discourse, will help others to influence and infiltrate this discourse. But to truly understand which structures of thought are in place, we will need to investigate much more and precisely beyond the content of the specific discourse. Not simply an understanding of discourses, we need to to understand epistemological knowledge, to become Foucauldian archaeologists.

It is important to note that discourse does not refer to a system of language, but a discourse always concerns itself as being an actual event in a specific context or situation. A discourse is always connected to people, and cannot be considered an abstract being. A discourse itself has no meaning, only for those within a discourse does a

52 See: Michael Walzer, *Spheres of Justice.*

discourse "refer to a world that it claims to describe, to express, or to represent."[53] A discourse is thus one that comes into action, and truth is an expression of the world which can only be expressed through a discourse, an action taking place in a time and space. Or, as Blanchot reminds us, a discourse is the world which "we untiringly construct [...] in order that the hidden dissolution, the universal corruption that governs what 'is' should be forgotten in favour of a clear and defined coherence of notions and objects, relations and forms".[54]

Discourse and Truth

Discourse is thus not only a network of referential terms which create meaning, it is also the place where truth can emerge. (We will come back to this when discussing Badiou's understanding of *world* and the manner in which truth comes into being according to his ontology.) Truth can only exist within a specific discourse and is only true for that very discourse. This does not limit truth to being subjective. Yet it would be correct to say that 'objective truth' is true for and under the premises of the specific discourse in which it is asserted.

In this respect, it is useful to look at one of the main metaphors known to Western thinking, namely the allegory of the cave which was introduced to us through the writings of Plato.[55] In this allegory reality is portrayed as the situation in which people are seated in a cave with their backs to the exit, looking at the shadows that are projected on the wall of the cave. These shadows are created by puppets, real objects that are held in the light of a fire that is lit within the cave. The cave is the allegory for the world, in which people are bound to the discourse they are in. They talk and take the play of shadows they see on the wall to be the truth. Trying to convince them that what they see are merely shadows is useless (and dangerous), as their understanding of 'truth' is based on their discourse.

53 Paul Ricoeur, *Text to Action*, p.145.
54 Maurice Blanchot, *The Infinite Conversation*, p.33.
55 Plato, *Republic*, Book VII.

Within their discourse, the world they create and through which they are created, the shadows are the truth. It makes no sense to deny this. And one could even say that hearing about something beyond the shadows is impossible. According to Plato's allegory, it is the philosopher's duty to stop thinking that this play of shadows is reality, to turn around and walk towards the exit of the cave in order to partake of the *Ideas*, the *Real* that is unknown to the people who are chained to the play of shadows. The philosopher then needs to go back into the cave and just like she was forcefully taken out of the slumber of the shadow-world, she must lead people out of the cave and into the light, the 'light' being the 'true' world that is outside the cave, the world of Ideas.

Although this is a very powerful allegory, there is something highly problematic about it. The assumption that the shadow-world in the cave is devoid of truth is mistaken. There is a community of people sharing a specific discourse, a network of referential terms, and therefore there is a situation where a group of people and their discourse point toward their own truth. For the philosopher, having seen the world of Ideas, this truth is no longer truthful, as he is no longer part of the same discourse. It is understandable for the philosopher to see the limits of the shadow-discourse as more limited than his own Ideas-discourse, as he can clearly see the link between the two. The light creates the shadows, and this is an insight the shadow-discourse does not have. Yet the philosopher returning into the cave, 'knowing' that other truth and perhaps even pitying the prisoners of the shadow-discourse, presenting her newly arrived at discourse as the 'truth' is herself unaware of the fact she is also limited to a specific discourse: a discourse in which light and shadow behave in a certain way, in which the shadows are no longer truth, but replaced by another set of truths. Who is to decide which 'truth' is higher or better or more worthwhile?

Although we need not consider the other implications of the idealist Platonic position, the cave-allegory clearly shows the way human beings are influenced by a specific discourse and how this brings about a specific understanding of truth. To try to break someone out of their own truth-bearing discourse (the shadows) and forcefully imprint them with another discourse (the Ideas), is a totalitarian gesture. It judges between different discourses and pretends they can be compared. We need to stay suspicious to any one discourse who claims mastery over another. Also, philosophy needs to be wary of producing these thoughts, as Badiou already pointed out, that "only philosophers have interiorized the notion that thought, *their* thought, encountered the historic and political crimes of this century and of all those leading up to it."[56] In other words, philosophers have a responsibility to not go along with the whims of the age in which they live, to impose any discourse as more important or as containing a higher truth than any other. At most we can conclude that each truth is true only within the context of the discourse from within which it emerged. And this emergence is not something merely given, it is an active creation on the part of the receivers, the ones who are themselves part and creating the discourse they inhabit. Deleuze confirms this, when he confronts philosophers with the fact that they prefer considering philosophy as a given knowledge, whereas "the concept is not given, it is created, has created; it is not formed, it places itself on itself, auto-positioning."[57]

It is important to look at Heidegger's ontological differentiation: a differentiation between the ontic level of that 'what is' (discourse) and the ontological level delineating the structures that inform and propagate that what is (episteme). This differentiation is crucial, as it links both 'levels' together. One does not exist without the other. There is no way of thinking 'being' without 'being' already there

56 Alain Badiou, *Manifesto for Philosophy*, p.28-29.
57 Gilles Deleuze and Félix Guattari, *Qu'est-ce que la philosophie?* p.16.

made present right in front of us. And at the same time, that what is presented to us is not limited to that what is made present, there is an underlying structuring at work to inform us of this being-present.

Paradigm and Weltanschauung

Defined in different discourses and fields of study, there are many terms used nowadays that refer to a specific set of views, thoughts and language that are limited to a certain group of users. In this regard, we can mention foremost the term 'paradigm', as it is popularly used and introduced by Thomas Kuhn. In a clarifying chapter written somewhat years after the appearance of his book *The Structure of Scientific Revolutions*, he distinguishes between two sets of usages of the word, the one being "global, embracing all the shared commitments of a scientific group; the other isolates a particularly important sort of commitment and is thus a subset of the first."[58] More particularly, Kuhn used the term 'paradigm' to delineate the "shared examples of successful practice"[59] of a particular group. Not so much the rules underlying the practice, but the instances in which the shared came into being, into the world. As such, we can note how this is exactly what I have referred to before as 'discourse' in that it is the being made visible, translated through what lies underneath – be it an unconscious or a conscious translation of the episteme (I will come back to this specific distinction later).

Another term used to describe an overarching group of discursive units, is *Weltanschuung* (world-view). Whereas an episteme can be seen as the total of possible ideas and structures of thought, a world-view is a specific and coherent set of understandings of the world at a specific time. As Heidegger notes: a *Weltanschauung* is "the basic attitude of people towards the totality of beings."[60] A worldview is

58 Thomas Kuhn, *The Essential Tension*, p.294.
59 Thomas Kuhn, *The Essential Tension*, p.318.
60 Martin Heidegger, *Holzwege*, p.93.

the basic attitude of people towards the totality of what is. But although this world-view, this image, is likened to a system, it is not merely a combination of what is. "To the essence of the picture belongs standing-together, system. By this, however, we do not mean the artificial, external simplification and collecting together of the given but, rather, the unfolding, developing unity of structure within that which is set-before, represented as such, which arises from the projection of the objectness of beings."[61] This world-view is a very personal one, as it is the link between what makes one human and what makes reality. What Heidegger refers to here as *Weltanschauung* is what I refer to as discourse.

Deleuze reiterates by voice of Nietzsche that it is important to realise that there is no such thing as a basis on which the can found our sense of reality, there is no *Grund*, there is no truth as such, although metaphysics has been searching for it for centuries. "All discourses, the scientific and philosophical ones included, are only prospects, or Weltanschauungen."[62] Discourse is all there is. Discourses are all we can lay our hands on when we want to figure out how the world around us and we ourselves function. Looking for anything beyond that is impossible.

Discourse and the Impossible

A discourse is a specific group of words, thoughts and rules which together form a conscious, accessible world for a specific group of people. We could thus say that a discourse or paradigm is a making visible, approachable, touchable, audible of that which is possible. Everything that is within the paradigm, within the discourse, is what is possible to be thought, seen, considered. Note here that something does not have to 'exist' according to a specific paradigm or discourse for that something to be part of the possible.

61 Martin Heidegger, *Holzwege*, p.100. Transl. Young & Haynes.
62 Gilles Deleuze, *Re-Writing Modernity*, p.6.

Take for example 'Pegasus'. A flying horse is not existent according to the laws of nature as we conceive of them. Yet we can imagine it, for instance as a drawing. Therefore, Pegasus is part of the conception of the 'possible'.

So, when we consider everything that is part of a discourse the possible, can we then conclude that everything that is not within a discourse or paradigm is the impossible? If that were true, we would simply have to think beyond the paradigm to reach the impossible. It is true that for something to be impossible, we need to locate ourselves outside of the discourses and paradigms present in society. But this is easier imagined than accomplished, as we are always already part of a discourse, by being human. One could even say that trying to reach for the impossible through the view of the possible is problematic in itself. But more on that later when we deal with framing the question of the impossible.

Changes Within Discourses: Non-Radical Changes

Most of the phenomena we call 'change' are actually mere instances of a rearranging of elements, a change of formats, a change within discourse. This makes sense, when we realise that we are thrown into the discourse we find ourselves in. The discourse marks the limits of our understanding, our thoughts, and comprises our network of truth references. The discourse prescribes along which categories we can think. The kind of change that takes place within a discourse does not involve the impossible, the beyond of the discourse, world, paradigm.

A change within a discourse or paradigm needs to be separated from fundamental or radical change. Changes within a discourse or even a change from one paradigm to another paradigm is not a radical change. As all discourses and all paradigms are informed by the episteme, a new paradigm by definition does not itself break the underlying understanding of reality. When giving a new answer to a question, changing from 'yes' to 'no', we remain in the same domain, in the same structure of how things can be thought. Radical change instead concerns itself with a change from one episteme to another, a change that involves a restructuring of basic notions that influence all aspects of our thinking and experiencing of reality. For now, it is enough to realise that a change within or between discourses will not bring us towards a notion of the impossible. And as this radical change is at stake here, that we have set out to investigate, we find our understanding of it continuously obstructed by the discourses we find ourselves in.

Badiou refers to this problem of mistakenly treating non-radical change as a seemingly radical change as a "mixture of conservation and partial imitation", as an 'academicism'.[63] This mistake allows for the eternal recurrence of what already is, bringing it to light again, thinking it again, without altering the parameters along whose lines one is thinking it. As Badiou acknowledges the need for a radical change, we will review his notion of 'world' and 'event' and discuss how these set out to account for a radical break within the world. It is however questionable whether his understanding of 'radical' change is truly reaching for the impossible. But let us first finish our discussion of discourses by looking into the phenomenon of language.

---

63 Alain Badiou, *Logics of Worlds*, p.73.

LANGUAGE

One of the most obvious manners in which to imagine a discourse, is to think of it as a language. Many authors have spoken about this before. Foucault conceived of language as discourse.[64] And Roland Barthes's analysis of discursive structures, "is complementary to Foucault's work, in that he too is concerned to describe the structures within which individuals in love are at the mercy of the tropes, moods, emotions, gestures, tones of voice which the discourse of the lover lays out for them. Barthes considers these structured elements to constitute what he calls 'fragments', which make up the discourse as a whole."[65]

Language is however not to be taken as synonymous to discourse, but is one specific type of discourse. "Even when linguistics claims to confine itself to what is explicit and to make no presuppositions about language, it is still in the sphere of a discourse implying particular modes of assemblage and types of social power."[66] Just like we always think of *a* language *within* a language when want to approach the mechanisms and characteristics of 'language'. The same goes for discourses. The framing of a discourse, the putting into language of that which is at most a desire, a direction, is therefore in itself a problematic issue that needs to be discussed.

Language itself is an apparatus, a mechanism that creates discourses, that limits and organises. There is nothing that is not always already also within language, as Benjamin has pointed out: "There is not something that happens or a thing either in the organic or inorganic nature, that is not in a specific manner part of language."[67] In that sense, language is always a saying of, a referring to what

64 See: Leonard Lawlor, *Thinking through French Philosophy*, pp.143-150.
65 Sara Mills, *Discourse*, p.55.
66 Gilles Deleuze and Félix Guattari, *A Thousand Plateaus*, p.7.
67 Walter Benjamin, *Gesammelte Schriften* II.i, p.140-141.

already is. Any uttering, any speech, is, through speaking it, taking a step away from that what is, it adds a level that comes between the observer and the observed. "And, certainly, when I speak, I recognize very well that there is speech only because what 'is' has disappeared in what names it…"[68]

Yet we cannot deny that one is always already present in language. "Man does not exist prior to language, either as a species or as an individual. We never encounter a state where man is separated from language, which he then elaborates in order to 'express' what is happening to him: it is language which teaches the definition of man, not the contrary."[69]

Whenever we imagine the impossible to be there, in an experience, in a moment, in a way that is beyond reckoning, the putting into language of this impossibility would kill it. Blanchot names the problem of finding a way of putting the question of the impossible, the most important question, the question of ontology, into language: "It has not found a language in which it can be said; the very language in which it speaks remains a language that belongs to the domain of what is."[70] Language is an instrument that establishes a secure reign, says Blanchot, as it covers over, rejects that which is outside of the discourse.[71]

Also Heidegger acknowledges the strain that the world and discourse puts on human being. "Man acts as though he were the shaper and master of language, while in fact language remains the master of man."[72] And: "What we speak of, language, is always ahead of us. Our speaking merely follows language constantly."[73] The discourses present in society thus control man, they limit and structure and

68 Maurice Blanchot, *The Infinite Conversation*, p.34.
69 Roland Barthes, *The Rustle of Language*, p.13.
70 Maurice Blanchot, *The Infinite Conversation*, Note 3, p.439.
71 See for instance: Maurice Blanchot, *The Infinite Conversation*, p.33.
72 Martin Heidegger, *Poetry, Language, Thought*, p.215.
73 Heidegger, *Unterwegs zur Sprache*, GA 12, p.179.

dictate what can be considered true. But for Heidegger this does not mean that man is a prisoner of language, of discourses. He adds: "When this relation of dominance gets inverted, man hits upon strange manoeuvres. Language becomes the means of expression."[74] Heidegger sees this as the specific task and station of the poet. After his early work, Heidegger seems to have been continuously intrigued by poetry, which he regards as "the responding in which man authentically listens to the appeal of language (…), that which speaks."[75]

What is important here, is that language itself is what speaks. Language as language is not a mere expression, not to be taken as just an activity of man. Language itself is the one that speaks.[76] Language here needs to be taken as the linguistic part of a discourse, that creates and shapes the possible, the world in which we consider ourselves to be. Although the discourse is the conscious level of the epistemic foundation, it is the discourse, and its language, that gives meaning and shapes thought. Language is the ultimate panopticon.

Yet does this mean that once we find ourselves in this discourse, this linguistic net of truth, that we are completely controlled and framed by it? Although Heidegger acknowledges that "[w]e are then, within language – and with language before all else,"[77] are we not completely controlled and left to the command of language and discourse? The possibility of breaking free from man's original being thrown into discourse is essential. The letting go of this being bound to the discourse one finds oneself in, is the central question in this work, in our quest for the impossible. Heidegger asks himself the question of being, which according to him has to be asked over and over again. It is a repetition of the same question, looking for an answer to a going beyond of the limits of being thrown, and the beginning of originality, of *Eigentlichkeit*. It is no wonder that Heidegger

74 Martin Heidegger, *Poetry, Language, Thought*, p.215.
75 Martin Heidegger, *Poetry, Language, Thought*, p.216.
76 Martin Heidegger, *Poetry, Language, Thought*, p.194.
77 Martin Heidegger, *On the Way to Language*, p.112.

looked into the phenomenon of language, which structures man's thinking as part of *das Man*, but which is at the same time also a way out of this being bound to the givenness of circumstance. Instead of trying to overcome this limit of language, Heidegger situates language as the place *par excellence* that appropriates the human being. It is poetry that voices language as language, instead of language as a mere expression, a representation. It is important to note that Heidegger writes that "everyday language is a forgotten and therefore used-up poem, from which there hardly resounds a call any longer."[78]

Heidegger thereby confirms that the discourse, the language within which we find ourselves, is not the most fundamental ground through which we understand reality. When we look as Heidegger's "*Der vorprädikative Charakter der Als-Struktur*,"[79] loosely translated as the pre-predicative character of the 'if'-structure, the seeing something as something, we notice there is something that precedes language. We already take the things as they are, before language (predicates, names) comes into play. The seeing of something as something[80] does not mean that through this 'if'-structure reality becomes '*ausdrücklich*', sayable, within the realm of language. Instead, this "un-say-ability is what creates the naivety of this pre-linguistic character."[81]

78 Martin Heidegger, *Poetry, Language, Thought*, p.205.
79 Martin Heidegger, *Logik*, p.144.
80 Martin Heidegger, *Logik*, p.145.
81 Martin Heidegger, *Logik*, p.145.

The Impossible, Beyond Language

For the early Wittgenstein, language is the totality of propositions. The world should be seen as the totality of facts that determine what is and what is not. It is the Foucauldian discourse, within which true and false can be distinguished. In this world, propositions picture an imagined model of reality, determining a place in the logical space which the specific fact establishes. It is therefore true that when we imagine a world that does not fit the facts, for instance when we consider an 'illogical fact' in a logical world, than we cannot imagine or 'say' what this world would look like.[82] Still, anything framed by and in language is already part of the world, even "an imagined world must have something in common with [this present world]."[83] It is important here to realise that with the term 'world', Wittgenstein refers to what we've termed 'discourse'. Wittgenstein tries to force an easy solution on the question of the impossible. He is right: it is one way of thinking of the beyond as non-sensical, unutterable in language. Any question of the beyond should then be banned to the mad-house or the realm of the mystical and be left alone when one wants to make sense of things, when one wants to deal with change and the desire for originality.

But there is another way in which to read Wittgenstein, namely by looking at the 'limits' he delineates. When Wittgenstein talks about 'the limits of my language are the limits of my world', he introduces the word 'limit'. As Puntel points out: "A limit is namely only that, when there is a dimension on the other side of the limit; to point at a limit of a or the language, means that a 'linguistic space' is entered"[84] Yet this is only true when we speak of a specific language, my language. But from language *an sich* one cannot break free. This 'not' is however not to be seen as yet another limit, as Puntel's main argu-

82 Ludwig Wittgenstein, *Tractatus logico-philosophicus*, §3.032.
83 Ludwig Wittgenstein, *Tractatus logico-philosophicus*, §2.022.
84 Lorenz Puntel, *Struktur und Sein*, p.41.

ment is that philosophy and the language it introduces as semiotic structure must be taken in a limitless sense. By doing so, he forcefully puts an end to the thinking about the impossible. Language as limitless structure becomes yet again a totalitarian force which frames human being. "The way we think and speak arises out of decisions our language has already made for us: language discreetly dictates to its users – in an invisible manner – self-evident assumptions and proscriptions that are inscribed in its grammar (which is, by definition, imperceptible from inside the language)."[85]

In the essay *Language as Such and Language of Man*, Benjamin points us in another, perhaps more fruitful, direction. For Benjamin, language is the linguistic being of things. Meaning is conveyed not *through* language, but *in* language.[86] Again we can see here that we find ourselves *in* language, and receiving meaning and those parts of reality which are part of this language-discourse insofar we can approach it. If we ask what it is that language conveys, we need to say that it conveys only itself. It is the mental being that it is, that it says. This is what Heidegger meant by language that speaks itself.

Benjamin doesn't limit reality to that which is conveyable *in* language. Instead, he says that whatever is unconveyable belongs to the main problem of linguistic theory, which he refers to as 'magical'.[87] And the realm of the magical is unlimited, except being limited by being unconveyable [*unmitteilbar*]. We will consider these things more thoroughly later, as the problem of language will become the main focus the third part of this book, when we confront the impossibility of voicing a desire for the impossible, which is problematic and simultaneously fundamental to this quest for the impossible. For now, it is important that the relation between language and discourses and the power they hold over truth and understanding has been established.

85 Shoshana Felman, *Writing and Madness*, p.18-19.
86 Walter Benjamin, *Gesammelte Schriften* II.i, p.142.
87 Walter Benjamin, *Gesammelte Schriften* II.i, p.142.

BADIOU'S WORLD & THE EVENT

Badiou gives us an insight into the direction he thinks philosophy must take. "A philosophy sets out to construct a *space of thought* in which the different subjective types, expressed by the singular truths of its time, coexist."[88] As I have described earlier, I do not agree with viewing philosophy as a method of description of 'what is', as philosophy's objective is to find a beyond of this so-called space of thought. This is however not merely a disagreement: it runs parallel to different understandings of what is meant by *world*.

This 'space of thought' to which Badiou refers, could be taken as an easy definition of what he first labelled 'situations' and has in his more recent work referred to as 'world'. A 'world', according to Badiou, is to be seen as a local site of the identification of beings.[89] What is important here is the word 'local': as, for Badiou, a *world* is singular, depending on time and place. "Every world is capable of producing its own truth within itself."[90] Every being that exists, is in reality the appearing of truth, in a world.[91]

For Badiou, *world* should be seen as a local, specific set of understandings, and can therefore be seen as a discourse or paradigm, as it includes a specific set of 'truths' and all their forms and modifications. As he puts it, "a world is the set of its modifications."[92] A discourse is the area in which truth arises, in a network of meaning-giving situations and referents. Therefore, we can understand the Badiouian 'world' as a discourse, in the sense of an arena of truth, a network of referents. So, we can say that Badiou sees philosophy as an outlining of discourse, of the outlining of the possible. The Badiouian world as the set of its modifications sees the world as a dis-

88 Alain Badiou, *Ethics*, p.28.
89 Alain Badiou, *Logics of Worlds*, p.113.
90 Alain Badiou, *Logics of Worlds*, p.8.
91 Alain Badiou, *Logics of Worlds*, p.36.
92 Alain Badiou, *Logics of Worlds*, p.359.

course within which a specific set of truths exists. For Badiou there is a multitude of truths, modifications that all belong to the set which is called 'world'. But this distinction doesn't make any difference in how worlds function – they follow the description of what we have defined here as discourse.

Badiou's Event & the Impossible

So, what does this mean for our search for the impossible, that what lies beyond the known and possible? How does Badiou consider the coming into being of radical change? It is exactly in order to think about the limits of understanding being that Badiou has introduced his whole set of distinctions, based upon a mathematical ontology. The distinctive feature that Badiou introduces is what he calls the 'Event', the place where there is an opening, a tear, in the texture of a situation.[93] It is this event that brings into being a newness, a world in which truth can appear. "The origin of a truth is of the order of the Event... In the beginning in the situation if no (pure) Event, supplements it, there is no truth, only veridicality."[94] It is the world that is created, shaped, by the Event, that bears the possibility, the opening of a truth. It is thus interesting to see how the Badiouian Event is a type of apparatus through which a world comes into its place.

Badiou seeks to take a closer look at these Events that exist "as exceptions to what there is".[95] He follows the classical distinction of Descartes, between substances – either thinking or extended – and truths. By doing so, he can start looking into the logical existence of truth. In order to do so, he wants to "examine the constitution, in singular worlds, of the appearing of truths, and therefore of what grounds the evidence of their existence."[96]

93 Oliver Feltham, *Alain Badiou: Live Theory,* p.101.
94 Alain Badiou, *Manifesto for Philosophy*, 36-7.
95 Alain Badiou, *Logics of Worlds*, p.5.
96 Alain Badiou, *Logics of Worlds*, p.9.

It is good to go back to what Badiou calls a world, namely: the set of its modifications. According to him, there are four types of empirical change, namely real change and modification, fact and (weak) singularity. Interesting here is the difference he makes between real change and modifications. Real change is that "which imposes an effective discontinuity on the world where it takes place". Modification refers to "the rule-governed appearing of intensive variations which a transcendental authorizes in the world of which it is the transcendental."[97] This means that any change in the sense of 'appearing-in-the-world' is an element of the multiplicity, of the world itself. A modification should therefore not be seen as 'change' according to Badiou. This is completely in line with our exploration of 'discourses' and how to understand changes within them. When we look for the emerging of the beyond, the impossible, we will need to look for what Badiou calls the Event, as modifications are always mere trans-formations of the present world.

Yet, when we consider true change as a coming into existence of something that was not previously existent, as something more than a re-organising of elements, we are faced with a paradox:

> There is a paradox in the idea of transformation. If a transformation is deep-seated enough, it might also transform the very criteria by which we could identify it, thus making it unintelligible to us. But if it is intelligible, it might be because the transformation was not radical enough. If we can talk about the change then it is not full-blooded enough; but if it is full-blooded enough, it threatens to fall outside our comprehension. Change must presuppose continuity – a subject to whom the alteration occurs – if we are not to be left merely with two incommensurable states; but how can such continuity be compatible with revolutionary upheaval?[98]

97 Alain Badiou, *Logics of Worlds*, p.359.
98 Terry Eagleton, *Figures of Dissent*, p. 246.

From a phenomenological perspective, a fundamental problem is issued here: How can the one who is subject to the change, who observes the change, account for this change? If he can connect to both the before and that what occurs after the change, there must be some overlap, some recognition that he as an observer is the same, a similar entity. But if we limit change as to what we can recognise as change, aren't we trying to postulate a non-true change? Are we back to pretending change to be merely modifications of the same?

How then can we, in a world which is mainly dominated by a material outlook on reality, argue how a true newness comes about? How can a 'something' come from 'nothing'? Perhaps the only area in which this topic might still be truly considered would be theology. In discussions in which posits 'the void' as the nothingness from which something completely new comes into being, and in which the appearing of the inexistent are central themes, it is difficult not to fall prey to quasi-spiritual terminology. Yet it is precisely this topic that Alain Badiou is presumably contemplating in his book *Logics of Worlds* (2009). Producing a language of his own, as seems to be an acceptable phenomenon among philosophers, Badiou is looking for a logic to explain how the inexistent comes into existence.

Badiou talks about events as the rupture in the world, as something that takes place and because of which new worlds and truths emerge. In order for this 'rupture' to take place, a void must be present in which place the new world can emerge. Before we start to look into what this void is, let us first consider if this is the right way to look to begin with, when we're truly after finding the impossible.

What is meant by 'new' world and truth? Is it the same as what we are aiming at when we want to define new as a beyond the already existing possible? Unfortunately Badiou is not talking about this sense of the new. I concur with Žižek, that Badiou is not looking for something radically new to emerge, for a beyond, a reaching for the impossible. As Žižek explains in an essay on Badiou: "The properly Hegelian enigma is here not 'how is an Event, the rise of something truly New, possible?', but, rather, how do we pass from Being to World, to (finite) appearance, i.e., how can Being, its flat infinite multiplicity, APPEAR (to itself)?"[99]

The reason why Badiou is not looking for a radical new, is that his understanding of 'world' is purely local and limited to the situation. 'World' for Badiou refers to the locally possible, and a world is constituted by the emergence of a truth. This is precisely the same as what happens in a discourse. A truth can only emerge in the situation of the references that make sense. Without a world/discourse, there is no possibility for truth to begin with. Also, whatever emerges, it becomes only a truth when it is within a world/discourse.

No Evidence for Rupture and the Impossible

Badiou introduces the necessity of a void for the emergence of a new. He argues that the coming into something new results from a void that is already present in the past, in the present-world and which makes the coming into being of the new possible. But is this then really a new, a coming-into-existence of that what was previously impossible?

No. The void for Badiou is related to the present world. The void already exists, latent and perhaps unconscious and even unrecognisable. The void for Badiou can only be pointed at, and can only be recognised afterwards. Yet the void is related to the present-world, it comes into being while depending and relating to the present-world, and as such cannot be separated from the frames and truths of the present-world. The void is not an out-of-this-world entity, not the complete lack of worldliness. It is part of the present-world.

99 Slavoj Žižek, *On Alain Badiou and Logiques des Mondes.*

Even if a new world can emerge from the rupture of the old, this does not mean a radical new emerges. As 'world' is a purely local site and a discourse a specific set, the movement from one discourse into the next does not make for reaching an impossible. There is no new episteme, no radically new that was not already present. Or at least there is nothing that warrants such a radicality.

The void which Badiou speaks of is only a void in relation to the world which is present. A void at this level is not a void in the sense of an emptiness that creates a severance of all relationships to what is. It is always already in relation to the old world, that this void emerged. There is no radical new emergence, not even the void itself is a radical new. What has come into being is only a new truth. And it is truth precisely and only because it is in relation to this world.

What is important to note is how Badiou's Event differs from fundamental change as a break from the old. For Badiou "posits that (…) the possibility of anything new occurring lies within the repetition of something old (…) [that] anything new is never completely different – it is a 'new world within an old world', an opening up of a radical space within the existing world."[100] In our quest for the impossible, this space that comes into being in an already existing world, is never radical enough to be considered a radical break. For Badiou there is thus no fundamental change independent from what was.

Therefore, the types of changes Badiou points at, are no more than changes within worlds, within paradigms, within discourses. This does not mean they are meaningless or devoid of worth. It does mean that our quest for the impossible has reached its endgame. In fact, the range of the impossibility of our quest might only now have become truly clear.

100 Jeremy Fernando, *Reading Blindly,* p.62.

Problem of Using Examples

Labelling Badiouian events as radical change is problematic for yet another reason, which has to do with his use of examples. The problem with using examples is that it refers to a specific world, a situation that is personal and local. These are for Badiou the only types of worlds that exist, so giving examples is by no means strange from his perspective. Yet whenever he describes an event that is situated in a local world, he makes so many presuppositions, that the exemplifying power of his examples is fallacious.

This has to do with the nature of language itself. When framing an event in language, we posit that which we refer to as 'impossible' into a framework of referents which only refer to that what already is. Even in the pointing towards the outside, we find ourselves already framed and placed among that what is possible, and nothing more. Let it suffice to say, that whatever already is, is never impossible. It might have been impossible at one point in time, yet we can in no way relate to this fully; the discourse at that time is forever beyond the limits of our understanding, of our discourse. So, we always look at this example from the perspective of the victor – of the discourse which has survived, which perhaps came into being precisely because of the 'change' that happened. In order to judge the Event, we look at it from this perspective, and understand it according to the categories which we presently inhabit. The example only has value within the discourse I'm presently in. It doesn't say anything and carries no meaning outside of the discourse. Any example of an Event is therefore an illusion – it is a temptation to try to come up with a solution as to how the present has come about. But when an Event is truly so life-changing, discourse-breaking, there will not be a trace left for us to observe as being an Event. This is the argument Eagleton already pointed out. And then we don't even look at the historical aspect to this problem, which we will explore later.

The problem of examples is only the beginning of a much larger problem, which is opened up by the question of the impossible. Perhaps Badiou's work is one more example of the extent to which discourses frames one's mind. As Lyotard reminds us: "Every discourse, including that of science or philosophy, is only a perspective, a *Weltanschauung*."[101]

However, Badiou acknowledges the risk that change, the truly beyond of what is, remains unthinkable. This has to do with the fact that an appearing remains beyond the control and understanding of the structures of thought. The appearing, the ontological figure of the instant has no other feature than that it appears only to disappear. The effects of this appearing are not part of the event itself, they are mere consequences. These effects are what make the event 'interesting' in hindsight. But this can never be a reason for labelling an event 'radical', going beyond the what-is.

101 Jean-François Lyotard, *The Inhuman: Reflections on Time*, p.28–29.

APPARATUS & GESTELL

Giorgio Agamben has written on what Foucault called 'apparatus' (*dispositif*). In an essay, he describes how the apparatus is a positive "set of beliefs, rules and rites that in a certain society and at a certain historical moment are externally imposed on individuals." As Foucault describes it:

> What I'm trying to single out with this term is, first and foremost, a thoroughly heterogeneous set consisting of discourses, institutions, architectural forms, regulatory decisions, laws, administrative measures, scientific statements, philosophical, moral, and philanthropic propositions – in short, the said as much as the unsaid. Such are the elements of the apparatus. The apparatus itself is the network that can be established between these elements...[102]

Whereas an episteme and a discourse make a distinction between the *ontic* and *ontological* level of knowledge, the apparatus is that mechanism that tries to link these levels of knowledge together as a network, as "a set of strategies of the relations of forces supporting, and supported by, certain types of knowledge."[103] This is of course related to the 'plays of power' that entails much of Foucault's work. The apparatus is the making visible of these plays of power, the set of practises and mechanisms in play in the world.

The apparatus is thus a "set of practices, bodies of knowledge, measures, and institutions that aim to manage, govern, control, and orient – in a way that purports to be useful – the behaviors, gestures, and thoughts of human beings."[104] In this it is similar to what Heidegger referred to as *Gestell.* Ge-stell (literally: to put in place) refers in Heidegger's thought to the enframing of being, "the

102 Michel Foucault, *Power/Knowledge*, p.194.
103 Michel Foucault, *Power/Knowledge*, p.196.
104 Giorgio Agamben, *What is an Apparatus?* p.12.

gathering together of that setting-upon which sets upon man, i.e., challenges him forth, to reveal the real, in the mode of ordering, as standing-reserve."[105]

This putting into place, this situating to reveal the real, is the mechanism that, according to Agamben, Foucault refers to when describing the apparatus. Turning to a critique of present society, Agamben shows us the relation between the apparatus and the subject, man in the world. The apparatus is a form of *oikonomia*, an economy which "realizes a pure activity of governance devoid of any foundation in being."[106] The apparatus, as we have just seen, is that which makes visible, which reveals in the world what is hidden underneath. The apparatus thus shows us an interesting relation to *man*. "Apparatuses must always imply a process of subjectification, that is to say, they must produce their subject", as Agamben tells us. Apparatuses as machines of subjectification are thus also "a machine of governance".[107]

The apparatus should be strictly distinguished from episteme and discourse, although its outcome regarding thinking the impossible is somewhat similar. The apparatus is not a descriptive, encompassing notion that describes the limits. It is much more a mechanism at work within the episteme, tailoring the resulting discourses according to its own whims. The apparatus accomplishes the unconscious intention of the episteme. "The techno-scientific apparatus which Heidegger calls the *Gestell* does indeed 'accomplish' metaphysics, as he writes."[108] The discourse is that set of enunciations that are the result of the translation of the unconscious episteme into a specific time and space, and the apparatus is the mechanism which performs that translation.

---

105 Martin Heidegger, *The Question Concerning Technology and Other Essays*, p.20.
106 Giorgio Agamben, *What is an Apparatus?* p.11.
107 Giorgio Agamben, *What is an Apparatus?* p.20.
108 François Lyotard, *The Inhuman*, p.69.

Apparatus and the Impossible

The apparatus is the translation of the episteme into discourses, the controlling mechanism that orients human beings. When we return to our original question, could it be that the apparatus can lead us to the impossible?

The apparatus is the crown on that which is existing. It lets the episteme flourish on a conscious level, it creates structures of governance and subjects, networks of meaning that are all based on the episteme. The apparatus makes visible what was previously not visible. But even though what is accomplished and made real through the apparatus was previously invisible, it was already existent. The pre-existent reality was already there, the set of the possible was merely not yet made explicit. Its power was latent, but inescapable. The apparatus works according to the underlying rules of the episteme.

But why can't there be an apparatus that makes the impossible visible? Let us imagine exactly such an apparatus that is solely designed to let the impossible surface. If thought of as a mathematical formula, we could say:

$$A(P) = I$$

with P=Possible, A=Apparatus, I=Impossible
and where the apparatus is a hitherto unknown function.[109]

The problem with this kind of reasoning is that it makes assumptions about the unknown impossible and limits the impossible before it is even in existence. This primarily has to do with the fact that the apparatus is a mechanism that can only deal with the already existent episteme. Even if it were to deny all of the episteme (i.e. $A = \neg P$), the resulting 'I' would still remain within the existing episteme. Negation is also a relationship, one that links the outcome to that

109 With thanks to Gabriel Yoran.

what is negated. The fact that it has a direct relation to the present episteme, makes it limited to that very episteme, at least by being directly related to it.

We can therefore conclude that the impossible is outside of the reach of the apparatus. In fact, the apparatus should be seen as an agent of the episteme, a framer of the discourse. It is the engine that powers the discourse, that makes it powerful enough to pull us in. With the apparatus there is still no beyond, there is only Gestell, the placing of the understanding of being.

CONCLUDING THE FRAME

Working our way through these previously established philosophical notions, we've come to the point that an encompassing frame of the 'what is' can be distinguished. But what does this frame mean, does it itself not already limit our understanding? Isn't this frame itself an apparatus, a framing within an episteme and contributing to a specific discourse? Are we framing ourselves by setting out a frame which defines precisely what we want to escape? Are we setting ourselves up to a crime we cannot but or perhaps never can commit, an escape which is inevitable as it is impossible? Let us first, before moving on towards a discussion of the framing of ourselves and the framing of the question, clarify the terminology we will use from now on.

As we have seen, the Badiouian 'world' is a specific instance of a discourse. From now on, whenever the word 'world' is used without explicit reference to Badiou, we take world in a Wittgensteinian sense, meaning "everything that is the case".[110]

The distinctions between *Gestell*, paradigm, episteme, discourse show us there are at least some pre-fixed structures, frames, out there, in the world, that influence our thinking. They are not something we find in the world, but they influence us to frame how we can see the world in the first place. All these notions show that there is no way to go beyond or to think a before of these frames, to think about a being-there which would be before these frames, or would even be completely devoid of it. When considering the episteme, that unconscious body of rules and thoughts which frames all our experiences as human beings, we must recognise that these frames are at most only partly influenced by ourselves. Even the idea of us being something, somewhere, somehow, is already a product of the

110 David Markson, *Wittgenstein's Mistress*, p.44. Ludwig Wittgenstein, *Tractatus logico-philosophicus*, §1.

episteme which through the apparatus made us think about it within the discourse within which we are formulating our thoughts.

Foucault acknowledges this when he says that: "power produces, it produces reality, it produces domains of objects and rituals of truth."[111] We are surrounded by these power structures, we are inside of them, we are because of them. Reality as we experience it, is not an objective being-there. Or to put it differently, reality might exist beyond the control of power-structures, the physical world may exist independent of us, but there is no way we can verify this, there is no way we can find out about that – the world is beyond our reach, except through the frames from within which we approach the world around us. The divide between what is and what is not, is created by power-structures, by the discourses that are present today, for the most part invisibly so. The tree that is standing outside of my window, starting to recover from winter and beginning to produce new leaves, may or may not be an externally given object. It may even be entirely my creation, a human conception. When Kant delineated human reason, he explicitly referred to certain structures (time and space) in human thinking that are not empirically given. Instead, they are given *a priori*, 'a pure form of sensible intuition.' Kant reminds us that the objects in time and space, these objects *in themselves,* "are not known to us at all, and that what we call external objects are nothing but mere representations of our sensibility, the form of which is space."[112] The *a priori* given structures however extend far beyond merely space and time. It was marvellous how Kant defined and separated all kinds of manners so that we could get a formal grasp at human *Vernunft*. Yet for our purposes, when we consider the epistemic features of the world, it would be folly to delineate only time and space among these pre-ordained structures, as the categories by which we think are also to be understood as structures that lie beyond our grasp.

111 Michel Foucault, *Discipline and Punish*, p.194.
112 Immanuel Kant, *Kritik der reinen Vernunft*, B45.

But does this mean that these structures exist beyond human intervention and that everything is therefore already given? In other words: can there be something beyond all this pre-arranged structure, or is the world always already what it is and will always be?

There are two extreme positions we might want to explore concerning this. The first would be that thought or being is independent of structures, i.e. to refute the existence of the power of the episteme; the second would argue all thought or being is structure. In the first case, the pre-existing structure is of no influence on human understanding, which would mean any thought is possible at all times, and under all circumstances. It is hard to imagine this is the case, as what one is thinking or can possibly think is clearly influenced by, for instance, matters regarding where one is born, in which time one lives and which information one has. People working in advertisement thrive on the possibility to influence one's thinking without the audience actually consciously noticing this. Even though we don't notice it, this doesn't mean there isn't a structure in place. Therefore, we should refute the first extreme; structures of thought (episteme, discourse, apparatus) are very much influencing our thinking. Even considering a child to be a *tabula rasa*, a blank slate that can become anything and everything, is already structuring that child among lines of what we consider to be possible. Even being left abandoned in a street without name, in a city that does not exist, that has and never will leave any trace in any history, is not a being left without place. The moment some relation is made, an initial step linking here and there, this relation creates meaning, creates structure, creates being-with, *Mitsein*.

The other extreme is a little more plausible. It is easy to consider all thought to be structure. It is as Wittgenstein argued, the limits of my language are the limits of my world.[113] According to him there is a limit to our thinking, which is put there only in and through language, and when we ask ourselves what lies beyond this limit, we will only find nonsense.[114] As we have already seen, the beyond, the impossible, is always beyond that which can be considered true. But this does not mean that his conclusion is valid, that we should be silent regarding that which we cannot talk about.[115]

When all thought is structure, this would mean that we are not able to influence our understanding at all, that the world has pre-ordained whatever our thoughts may be. If this would be true, the reaching for the beyond would be nonsense not only according to rules of veracity, but also when considered from an ethical point of view. Change, the looking for a new, would only be possible in a way that is predictable and any such change would be limited to being a mere re-shuffling of what is already present. Some scientists and statisticians might assume that the world actually works like this. Current governments, be they dictatorial or democratic, would very much be in favour of a *demos* that is completely predictable and controllable. For now, we cannot completely rule out this possibility, that everything is already as it is, and that there is no breaking free of the structure that is always already here. But this doesn't mean our trying to find a beyond, the impossible, is devoid of merit. In a world in which everything is predetermined, structured and fixed, the search for the beyond is probably even the only important thing that remains. It is this struggle of reaching for a beyond that is impossible that is the basis of art and of philosophy.

113 Ludwig Wittgenstein, *Tractatus logico-philosophicus*, §5.6.
114 Ludwig Wittgenstein, *Tractatus logico-philosophicus*, Vorwort 1918.
115 Ludwig Wittgenstein, *Tractatus logico-philosophicus*, Vorwort 1918.

It would be useful to find historical examples of events that reached this beyond-the-possible, something we might refer to as 'radical change', in order to show how change works and to clear up this matter once and for all. If we can prove a beyond can or could once be reached, radical change would become possible, and we would no longer find ourselves in a world from which no escape is possible.

Unfortunately things are not that simple. As described before, there is a fundamental problem with any example we might find, as any example is foremost exemplifying our present discursive understanding of the world. At the very moment we recognise something as a beyond, as an impossible, we are already looking at it from within a frame. And this problem relates not only to examples, but to anything we might claim to be true. The fact that I can understand, give meaning to an instant, an event, means that that what I observe or refer to is already part of the world I inhabit. This is what I would call the problem of already been framed myself.

FRAMING MYSELF

> "During the first days that followed our return, we were all, I think, seized by a veritable delirium. We wished to speak, to be heard at last. And yet it was impossible."
> ~ Robert Antelme, *The Human Race*

Even when we've delineated the frame of the possible, once we've put into position [*Ge-stell*] that which is, we are faced with the problem of our own being. Describing the frame, even on a meta-level, is only possible from within the frame in which we already find ourselves. It is the problematic fact of me doing the looking. Whatever I write, no matter how many other thinkers and perspectives I evoke, any description is already part of a specific world, even a specific episteme and discourse – whether I am conscious of it or not. Whatever I read, I can only read it inasmuch as I already know it, relate to it. Whatever I hear, see, notice – all is limited to what I already know. How can I deal with this already being stuck in a world? Am I confined by language, already always, despite my manoeuvres of trying to go beyond this?

When I want to come up with a notion of the possible and the impossible that is as devoid of a specific world as possible, the most I can do is to look into conceptions of reality and its genealogy. But even when working my way through a genealogy, deconstructing it, it is still me, making sense of it all. Or, to put it even more bluntly: whatever step I take, I have not taken one that leads me outside my own world. It is still me, with my rational possibilities and my eyes that are framed and shaped and following the rules of the present discourse that inform my every step. Somehow, I will have to accept this limitation, acknowledging the failing of any longing for a beyond-myself.

In other words, I am forced to focus on what I already am, what is already part of me. Focusing on this specific and limited part of the whole of human thinking is not so much due to circumstances, but a necessity. As I am born, raised and still living in my specific world, I am grounded in a specific tradition. Trying to fore-go this relationship would be doomed to fail. This is due to the fact, that the paradigm in which I find myself cannot be evaded. Or, as Maurice Blanchot would say, "We have always already begun, always already spoken. This 'always already' is the meaning of every beginning that is only a beginning again."[116]

One recent objection to this line of thinking comes from the field of (speculative) realism.[117] Its proponents propose a way out of language by making human understanding of the world merely one type of relationship between things, a relationship that is not higher or better than any other relation between objects. Yet this is not the issue here. Even when the speculative realist theory could account for everything that is, and every relation between it, the questions that deal with human life will not be addressed. Or will only be addressed by accounting for the human relations that are dependent on language as a relationship. As Wittgenstein says, "we feel that even when all *possible* scientific questions have been answered, the problems of life remain completely untouched."[118] Science, that domain of describing, understanding all that is, all that is possible, is the domain of (speculative) realism. But the question of the beyond is always a human one, as it is the beyond, the impossible, for the human being. The emergence of being that is totally unrelated to what is, is in a sense beyond the realism/idealism opposition.

116 Maurice Blanchot, *The Infinite Conversation*, p.16.

117 See: Quentin Meillassoux, *After Finitude*, and Graham Harman, *The Quadruple Object*.

118 Ludwig Wittgenstein, *Tractatus logico-philosophicus*, §6.52.

As Laclau and Mouffe put very elegantly:

> The fact that every object is constituted as an object of discourse has nothing to do with whether there is a world external to thought, or with the realism/idealism opposition. An earthquake or the falling of a brick is an event that certainly exists, in the sense that it occurs here and now, independently of my will. But whether their specificity as objects is constructed in terms of 'natural phenomena' or 'expressions of the wrath of God', depends upon the structuring of a discursive field. What is denied is not that such objects exist externally to thought, but the rather different assertion that they could constitute themselves as objects outside any discursive condition of emergence.[119]

119 Ernesto Laclau and Chantal Mouffe, *Hegemony and Socialist Strategy*, p.108.

BEING AS BEING-THROWN-IN-THE-WORLD

The problem with disclosing the world in which an event happens, is that this world itself is not an object of understanding. Whenever we approach a situation, an object, a concept, we will form an understanding of this object based upon the historical and transcendental pre-structure that we find ourselves is. This *thrownness* is the original situation in which we find ourselves, always.

Let us trace the Heideggerian approach to accounting for being-in-the-world before even any other notion can come into being: "as existent we already understand world beforehand."[120] For Heidegger, *Dasein* cannot be thought separate from the world. This means he doesn't make a Cartesian subject-object distinction, yet without conflating the two. Human life is a being-becoming (*advenir*) by being-in-the-world, which is also the starting point for that being.

'World' is therefore not a given reality outside of Being. "Space is not to be found in the subject, nor does the subjective observe the world 'as if' that world were a space; but the subject (*Dasein*), if well understood ontologically, is spatial."[121] Being itself is worldly, taking space, and simultaneously temporal – as Kant already pointed out. Both time and space are part of the foundation of *Dasein*.[122] *Dasein* is this firmly grounded in the episteme. "*Dasein* is a singular, unique possibility of making/letting an ownmost sense of the world and/or the world of an ownmost sense open itself."[123] This relation to the world, is what Heidegger refers to with a falling into the world [*Verfallenheit*], which is not to be seen as a negative, as it is also what creates the ontological being of *Dasein*. It is both historical as

120 Martin Heidegger cited by Julian Young, *Heidegger's Philosophy of Art*, p. 32.
121 Martin Heidegger, *Sein und Zeit*, p.111. Transl. Macquarrie & Robinson.
122 Martin Heidegger, *Sein und Zeit*, p.367.
123 Jean-Luc Nancy, *The Being-with of Being-there*, p.3.

a worldly aspect of falling, within which we can distinguish between *eigentlichem* and *uneigentlichem Sein*. When we merge ourselves with the world we are lost to it. Heidegger refers to this as how *Dasein* "... has mostly the character of Being-lost in the publicness of the 'they'."[124] This being lost is the being thrown, the dislocation of the being-self.[125] "*Dasein can* fall only *because* Being-in-the-world understandingly with a state-of-mind is an issue for it. On the other hand, *authentic* existence is not something which floats above falling everydayness; existentially, it is only a modified way in which such everydayness is seized upon."[126]

For Heidegger being is a dwelling-in-the-world. He traces this to the etymological origin of *innan-habitare-wohnen*, which in English means to dwell, "'*Ich bin' besagt wiederum: ich wohne, halte mich auf bei ... der Welt*"[127]: The 'I am' is again the I live, I dwell in the nearness, in, the world. But Heidegger also traces the etymology of being to '*buan*', building. Building is part of the original meaning of being, being-in-the-world.[128] Interestingly enough we can still find traces of this even in other languages, of the word 'habit' (English) and '*gewoonte*' (Dutch), both referring to the word 'to live' (*habitare/wonen*) and used in the context of the everydayness, the living the life in a place that one occupies. Dwelling is the basic attitude of human *Dasein* ("*den Grundzug des menschlichen Daseins*"[129]). And it is the house of language that human being occupies.

124 Martin Heidegger, *Sein und Zeit*, p.175. Transl. Macquarrie & Robinson.
125 Martin Heidegger, *Sein und Zeit*, p.178.
126 Martin Heidegger, *Sein und Zeit*, p.179. Transl. Macquarrie & Robinson.
127 Martin Heidegger, *Sein und Zeit*, p.54.
128 Martin Heidegger, *Vorträge und Aufsätze*, p.149.
129 Martin Heidegger, *Vorträge und Aufsätze*, p.193.

The question then arises, whether my fascination with the topic of the beyond, of a possibility of a radical other, a radical change from what we know as the realm of the present-possible, could even be considered original: is it not merely a product of my time? And especially when considering the topic of radical change, is it not merely a longing of this time and discourse within which I find myself, of individualism and a longing to move beyond nihilism, that this topic can even be brought up? In other words, how can a philosopher know she is not merely satisfying her own personal human longing, her desire for change as it is prescribed in the world she inhabits, when formulating a conception of the beyond, of radical change?

It is as Nietzsche already remarked about the profession of philosophy: "[i]t always creates the world in its own image, it cannot do otherwise; philosophy is this tyrannical drive itself, the most spiritual will to power, to 'creation of the word', to *cause prima*."[130] It is this desire, this will, an invisible spell under which philosophers "always trace once more the identical orbit: however independent of one another they may feel, with their will to criticism or systematism, something in them leads them, (…). Their thinking is in fact not so much a discovering as a recognizing, a remembering, a return and home-coming to a far-off, primordial total household of the soul out of which those concepts once emerged…"[131]

Even Nietzsche acknowledged how everything one writes, what every philosopher has hitherto been occupying herself with, that each philosophy is "a confession on the part of its author and a kind of involuntary and unconscious memoir…"[132] He refers to this as an intuition, nothing but a framing of the world in which the phi-

130 Friedrich Nietzsche, *Beyond Good and Evil*, p.39.
131 Friedrich Nietzsche, *Beyond Good and Evil*, section 20, p.50.
132 Friedrich Nietzsche, *Beyond Good and Evil*, section 6, p.37.

losopher finds herself. One is driven by these instances, which are beyond one's control, beyond consciousness. To consider one to be outside of these drives is just as ludicrous as thinking the thinking subject without acknowledging she is already thinking when the first thought is produced. There is no escape from the already present, the pre-structured world. As Wittgenstein confirms, I am my world. Were I to write a book about 'the world', I would need to write my own life into it.[133]

We can find the same acknowledgment of the dependence of thinking upon one's own world in some Eastern perceptions. The longing towards the beyond, the change, involves understanding the continuous process of having and letting go, 'the Way', in which the warning that Nietzsche was voicing can also be heard. The beyond can only be found when we agree with the idea that "we all remain fundamentally homeless. The Way keeps going further. 'Wu-shu' or 'do not abide' in English: do not settle down somewhere. We are nowhere at home."[134] But does any 'Way' which leads to a beyond, not at the same time starts from the now, the present, the world in which we find ourselves? How then can it ever reach the impossible?

Even our concept of time is discursively grounding us in what we always already know. As Lyotard reminds us, "...historical periodization belongs to an obsession that is characteristic of modernity."[135]

As such this text itself is fully grounded in today's *leitmotiv:* the longing for the beyond. The search for a breaking might be in vain. It might be a product of our paradigm and as such it will perhaps be impossible to use it as a starting point for the finding of an 'objective' mechanism or apparatus that results in the possibility of a break. And if we did find a break, a rupture, would it mean we have created it ourselves to satisfy our own needs? Would it be a mere illusion,

133 Ludwig Wittgenstein, *Tractatus logico-philosophicus*, §5.63-5.631.
134 Ton Lathouwers, *Zen Talks*, p.71.
135 François Lyotard, *The Inhuman: Reflections on Time*, p.25.

only meaningful in relation to the present world we find ourselves in? And if we don't find the possibility of fundamental change, what would that mean? Would it tell us something about the limits of our present paradigm, or does it say something about the most fundamental structure of truth and reality itself? Is it simply a curse of our time, to try to take modernity to the next level, or is it not so much a reflection of the limits of our own contemporary thinking but of the limits of human thinking in general? Or are we in this philosophical exercise merely repeating what countless others have done before us?

Or, as Cioran put it so wonderfully, are we just repeating a nonsensical breaking of the episteme, for a new one to emerge from the rubble? : "Each historical epoch is a world in itself, closed off and certain of its principles, until the dialectic movement of historical life creates a new, equally limited and deficient form."[136]

As Badiou writes in his preface to his reading of Wittgenstein, the "conditions of philosophy, i.e., the truths to which it bears witness, are always contemporary to it. It is in the confusion of their own time that philosophers construct new concepts, and they cannot diminish their alertness, be content with what is already there, or contribute to maintaining the status quo, without at the same time falling prey to the worst possible risk for the fate of their discipline: its absorption or incorporation into academic knowledge."[137] The process Badiou describes here, is the same for any movement which searches for the beyond. It is from a clash that this longing emerges, but this is always already contemporary, limited and framed by the time which produces it. The risk Badiou warns us about is not only a risk for philosophers, it is just as true for artists and scientists.

In the art world, the same thing happens. Any artist that creates, that shapes something, brings something into reality that was

136 Emil Cioran, *On the Heights of Despair*, p.66.
137 Alain Badiou, *Wittgensteins' Antiphilosophy*, p.67.

previously non-existent, enjoys a freedom and a possibility of the beyond. The moment that her work is named, labelled as a specific movement, framed within a discourse, the art as a movement of the beyond has disappeared. Perhaps it can still be seen in the original artwork, that first raised eyebrows, that stopped the beating of the throbbing heart of the present discourses. But when the artist herself frames her work within the discourse thus presented by her, through or for her, even when at first she had attained a beyond, by framing it within the discourse she is unable to reach that beyond again.

Nietzsche tells us the same, referring to artists who are no longer independently in the world and against the world, "*stehen lange nicht unabhängig genug in der Welt und gegen die Welt, als dass ihre Werthschätzungen und deren Wandel an sich Theilnahme verdiente!*"[138] Here he warns us to be aware that even artists aren't independent of the world, against the world, that their orientation and life often don't make it worthwhile to be considered as an *example* of a beyond.

It is not strange that in biographies of those whom we can feel an embodiment of the trace of this quest for the impossible, these labels of belonging to a specific reality, to established discourses are purposefully shunned. Which probably contributed to their early deaths and general poorness. The longing to belong to the respected milieu which Badiou referred to as the academy, is in those people overcome by a stronger longing to the beyond of the present. No acceptance by the world, is perhaps a prerequisite to truly go beyond that world. Nietzsche takes this even further when talking about philosophers. He says that philosophers should even withstand the word '*Wahrheit*' [*philos*, Truth] as philosophers are aware that "... whosoever possesses, will be possessed."[139]

138 Friedrich Nietzsche, *Zur Genealogie der Moral*, p.362.
139 Friedrich Nietzsche, *Zur Genealogie der Moral*, p.372-3.

FRAMING THE QUESTION

"…it seems that we question more than we are able to question, more than the power of questioning allows, and thus beyond the reach of any question."
~ Maurice Blanchot, *The Infinite Conversation*

Realising we already find ourselves in a world, occupying a framed space, the next problem we are faced with, is the way the question which we ask ourselves is framing the outcome.

Setting forth a question that asks what lies beyond all that can be thought and answered is impossible. At least this is true for Wittgenstein as he remarked, "When the answer cannot be put into words, neither can the question be put into words. The riddle does not exist. If a question can be framed at all, it is also possible to answer it."[140] Yet it is still valid to ask for that which cannot be said, when it concerns matters that may or may not be put into words. Wittgenstein refers to this specific domain as the mystical,[141] for Benjamin this is what is called magical.[142] But accepting this beyond as mystical or magical and not of the world, is not satisfying. It does not bring us closer to the impossible, instead it leaves it beyond consideration. It labels it and is done with it – whereas we are only starting to understand the magnitude of the question.

Therefore, let us explore how putting our question into language already demystifies the question itself. The question concerns a radical other, a fundamental change, a longing for the beyond. This desire present in us and in society, consists of a longing towards becoming. It could even be said that the longing towards authentic becoming is part of human nature. But what is human nature, but a construction? Even when no other conception can be deemed possible, this does

140 Ludwig Wittgenstein, *Tractatus logico-philosophicus*, §6.5.
141 Ludwig Wittgenstein, *Tractatus logico-philosophicus*, §6.522.
142 Walter Benjamin, *Gesammelte Schriften* II.I, p.142.

not make this specific understanding of what human nature is 'correct'. Correctness, truthfulness, is only possible within the framework we find ourselves in. The frame we inhabit speaks through us, but it is not us, it is the frame and its linguistic faculty, that speaks.

Therefore, we consider again, what is this question that is posed. What does it imply, to ask for the beyond? It asks to put this initial desire into words: Can there be a new? Is there originality possible? Originality as that which does not find its origin in that what precedes it. In other words: is the world framed in such a way, that we can only succumb to it? And it is precisely in language, within which we posit this question, which frames us, and which is used to search for a way to move beyond it. Language and its already-always-framing character should not be allowed to stop us. We are not going to give up on the project of looking for something beyond the world as we already know and see it. We are facing an age-old paradox. One that was already set forth in Plato's *Meno*, albeit in a somewhat different form. Can we look for something 'new', 'different' from what is already known, outside of the episteme? Could we ever see it?

In the dialogue between Meno and Socrates, as delivered to us through a text by Plato, Meno asks how we can recognise something without already knowing it. When we go out and search for a particular thing, or if someone tries to teach us a new concept, how can we know that what we've found, is actually what we were thinking of? "…If you come right up against it, how will you know that it's the unknown thing you're looking for?"[143]

Meno might as well have asked Socrates about desiring change, about how revolutions come to be, or how to break away from the shackles of everyday life. The answer would remain the same. Everything that is out of the ordinary, everything that lies beyond that what is already present, known, realized, is impossible to even search for.

143 Plato, *Meno*, 80d.

Yet what does Meno's paradox tell us? Again, it seems that the question of the new, the impossible, is one we need to let go of. Yet even though the question of the impossible might seem straightforward and impossible to answer, this does not mean we have come to the point in which we can simply let it go. After all, this question of breaking with the present, searching for the beyond, is referring to a desire present in society, in the human subject, in me. We cannot simply let go of this fundamental longing, but we can ask ourselves what it means to put this longing into a question. Does questioning this very question make answering impossible?

QUESTIONING THE QUESTION

Even the movement of a question itself is problematic. "To question is to seek, and to seek is to search radically, to go to the bottom, to sound, to work at the bottom, and, finally, to uproot. This uprooting that holds on to the root is the work of the question."[144] To question that what is possible, known, is to also hold on to the root of it. Posing the question, even when it is the right question, as the starting point of philosophy, might thus be a method that already creates the frame along which we can think, along which the answers can come as it holds on to the very root of what is present. Questioning is in itself already giving a direction. In questioning lies that what is intended to be questioned, and the question itself has thus already a relation to its own character of being, as Heidegger would put it.[145]

We thus need to look for a questioning that is not already bearing the answer in itself. A questioning that doesn't presuppose the frame of what is, but is neither a negation of that frame, as that would create the same relationship to that frame of what is, albeit negatively.

This other type of questioning itself could thus be seen as an example of how to attain the impossible. How can we both question, voice our concern regarding the impossible as a beyond of what is, but at the same time acknowledge that this questioning itself is always also fundamentally grounded in tradition, in something that has already been there for centuries and centuries.

There is an important aspect to the Jewish tradition of questioning, which concerns the way thoughts are invoked. Here questioning is not to be seen as a dialectical process, but as a true means of inquiry. On the one hand within this tradition it is recognised that there is a need for reinterpretation and a continual personal

144 Maurice Blanchot, *The Infinite Conversation*, p.11.
145 Martin Heidegger, *Sein und Zeit*, §2, p.5.

experience of the world and the phenomena in it. On the other hand, it is deemed improper to present this reinterpretation as if one has changed or added anything to what was already present.

Examples can be found for instance in the emergence of the Zohar, presented as the wisdom of old, and in that sense nothing new, but only a redoing of what was already known. Kabbala itself means 'tradition'. Whereas 'kabbala' is nowadays known in new age circles as an original method for spirituality, within the Jewish world it should not be seen as a new, but as yet one more way of approaching the old. It is a questioning anew, with a fresh mind, unencumbered by tradition, but at the same time fully aware that one is moving within the tradition. It is simultaneously holding on to the very things it un-does. This manner of questioning and repetition is developed further by Deleuze, to which we will return later.[146]

Desiring the Impossible

When desiring the impossible, we are asking for a specific type of thinking that is completely opening the present, leaving no trace of its origin.

To think is to question everything. To question requires that something happens that reason has not yet known. Non-Western traditions of thought have a quite different attitude. What counts in their manner of questioning is not at all to determine the reply as soon as possible, to seize and exhibit some object which will count as the cause of the phenomenon in question. But to be and remain questioned by it, to stay through meditation responsive to it, without neutralizing by explanation its power of disquiet.[147]

146 See for instance: Gilles Deleuze, *Difference and Repetition*.
147 Jean-François Lyotard, *The Inhuman*, p. 74.

This questioning deals with the acceptance of the disquiet, the willingness to risk everything that has given a stable footing, that has grounded us in being, to risk all that makes us a being. It is a questioning that leaves us devoid of any way of finding our way back to reality, to an ease of mind.

Blanchot reminds us that the ultimate question can only arrive at the moment in which the fullness of the discourse is affirmed. It is at that moment that we find the real question. "Thus, we understand why today, when the dialectic takes possession of everything, this necessity of questioning that presses upon us by bearing us toward the question of the whole also presses upon us by insistently drawing us into this question that is not posed; a question we will call, in defiance, in derision and with rigor, the most profound question—or the question of the neutral."[148]

148 Maurice Blanchot, *The Infinite Conversation*, p.18.

CONCLUDING THE FRAME

"All he [man] needs is the fortitude not to give up the search."
~ Socrates, Meno (Plato)

Placing and framing terminology that has hitherto been used and misused by many different philosophers, is only a first clearing of the throat. It creates a common ground, a shared understanding from which we may now rid ourselves altogether.

In order to conclude, let us look at the concept of 'world', and how it relates to the frame that we have constructed so far. According to Puntel, the concept of 'world' has been used in three different ways in contemporary philosophy.[149]

(1, Plato) World as collection of all beings, taken into account that the absolute being (the highest, the first, etc.) is not enclosed within the world, but world-transcendent.

(2, Kantian) World as radical dichotomy with the transcendental subjectivity. World is thus the totality of things which are unknowable to us.

(3, analytical) World is everything that is or exists. In general, (3a) world refers to being or 'universe of discourse', but it can also be used to describe a more specific *world* (3b), belonging to a specific point of view on what exists – for instance only physical entities.

In this last sense (3b), one is also able to speak of possible worlds. It should be clear that these possible worlds don't refer to a universal notion of 'world', but to something that Puntel calls 'actual world'.[150]

The way we will use the notion of 'world' is closest to the third, universal meaning. World encloses everything that is. It includes all beings (1) but also that which is referred to as world-transcendent,

149 Lorenz Puntel, *Struktur und Sein*, p.330-2.
150 Lorenz Puntel, *Struktur und Sein*, p.332.

the Platonic Idea, God. It includes that what is unknowable to us (2), but also acknowledges that the unknowability *for* the transcendental subject is already a relation, something which is also part of the world.

Therefore, we can say that world is both that which is in language and that what lies beyond language. World includes both the ontic and the ontological levels of being. Studying the world, delineating its parameters and limits, would be an archaeological enterprise as outlined by Foucault, yet our conclusions and our understanding and acknowledging of what it is that makes this world would be limited by the episteme, the epistemic space that fills the world. This epistemic space is not what makes the world in its fullest sense. Here we need to follow the Heideggerian insistence that there is 'reality', an "ontic persistence outside of ontological disclosure."[151]

It is thus that it must be clear that we need to distance ourselves from notions of 'world' that refer to discourses, which is the case in both Wittgenstein and Badiou. When Wittgenstein refers to 'my world' in that the limits of my language mean the limits of my world, he is not talking in a mere linguistic sense. His world is however a discourse, and one's language is always limited by the discourse one finds oneself in, or the combination of discourses that make up one's individual inhabited space. Equally, the Badiouian world as the set of the modifications, the totality of instances, or possibilities that can be uttered and are related, is to be understood as a discourse.

World is necessarily limitless. There is no beyond the world, at least not as long as the world *is*. Therefore, the world needs to be limitless, without beginning or end. Whenever the concept of world is used, we must be aware that "it is always in the middle, between things, interbeing, intermezzo."[152]

151 Slavoj Žižek, *Less than Nothing*, p.196.
152 Gilles Deleuze and Félix Guattari, *A Thousand Plateaus*, p.25.

What is left for us now is to shatter the world, the possible. When nothing remains, the impossible might come to light. Although there won't be any light remaining for us to label it, to understand it. Whenever the impossible approaches, it needs to hide to remain true to its being impossible.

Looking for this impossible, we are faced with a problem that was already understood by Heidegger: in talking about what is, we go beyond what is considered rational and understandable, which is why his later work is sometimes taken as a movement away from philosophy.[153] But it is in this movement and only through this movement that we can stay true to our desire towards the impossible. If we would stay within an understanding of philosophy as a description of the world, we would be faced with useless questions such as "Where are you going? Where are you coming from? What are you heading for?"[154]

We will not be heading anywhere except to failure. Yet we will map the desire for the impossible, and let us be led by it. To be human.

153 Lorenz Puntel, *Struktur und Sein*, p.559.
154 Gilles Deleuze and Félix Guattari, *A Thousand Plateaus*, p.25.

PART II

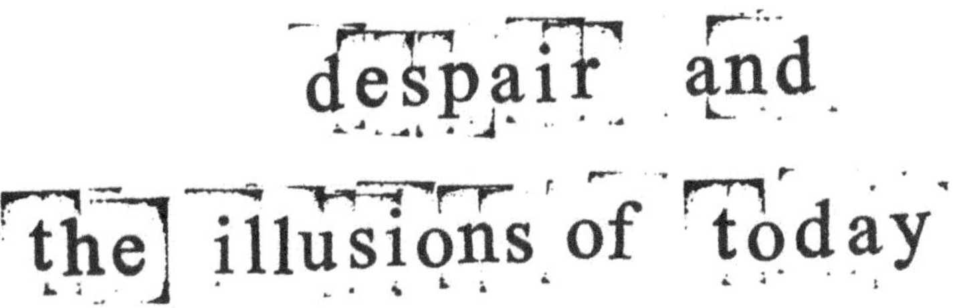

Being framed by our own thoughts, is there still hope? Can our desire for the impossible lead us anywhere despite the despair of knowing the outlines of the prison we call reality? And when we find a way out, how do we make sure that we haven't created one more illusion to make us think we have found an answer?

INTRODUCING THE DESPAIR

> "Intellectual despair results in neither weakness nor dreams, but in violence. It is only a matter of knowing how to give vent to one's rage; whether one only wants to wander like madmen around prisons, or whether one wants to overturn them."
> ~ Georges Bataille, *Visions of Excess*

It is time to take a break from the formal structures that definitions point us toward. It is time to pause ourselves from becoming entangled in the frame that has framed the world. To undo all the traces that have wrapped themselves around me, that have framed my mind. If I don't, the frame will be all there is, which is always already the case. What's left of me? Am I reduced to these words that circumambulate the meaning of the world which in itself have been designed according to those very same words?

I force myself to work through language despite language. In a language that is not my own, without translating my thoughts. Forming my thoughts simultaneously in all language, in all languages that are available to me. That are not merely signs without signifying anything. Quoting original thought from others, knowing that they are as inaccessible to me as to the other that reads it. Knowing also, that there is no such thing as an original. That understanding of the other is an illusion. Instead I can only understand myself better, framing and tying myself ever tighter to the frame that I am inhabiting.

DESIRE

Step by step, one foot at the time, I move forward, which is also backwards. I've framed the frame. I've traced, I've delineated the possible, that what can be known, the 'what is'. The impossible is however still beyond reach, my reach. There are many indications that it will remain beyond my reach, by the sheer fact of me being human. Human as beyond animal, but inside the frame that is humanity: the frame that is time and space. I find myself trapped within the possible, always already made possible by being thrown into this that is. Every thought, every utterance, sound, other, everything is already what is and what cannot but be.

Yet there remains this desire… This ultimate longing to cross the threshold of existence…

To desire. To want, to long, to crave, to need, to wish, to request, to dream, to yearn, to lust. For something, always something that is located outside of the self, myself, always on the other side of the line, beyond my reach. From the stars,[155] sidereal, that is, *de sidere*, the outer worldly, that which we can never reach. Once I obtain it, once it has come within my reach, my object of desire has ceased to be precisely that.

Desire for the beyond, ultimately desiring the *Other*. The radical other, who is impossible to be, to exist, to see, to approach. Underneath the other as my mirror-image, "there always lurks the unfathomable abyss of radical Otherness, of one about whom I finally know nothing…"[156]

155 Anne Dufourmantelle, personal conversation, Saas-Fee, 2013.
156 Slavoj Žižek, *How to Read Lacan*, p.43.

Even God, that Almighty Beyond that has occupied the minds of man for centuries, that notion to distract me from the abyss, the One that creates, the One that makes sense of it all, lies within our reach and therefore can never be the beyond any longer... as "he allows for a point of definition, limits."[157]

The desire for the impossible is thus my first desire, the primordial, the fundamental desire that creates the tension between myself as a human being and my incapability with being at ease with precisely that which it means to be: human. It is this desire that both gives life and that destroys any consolation I might find. My desire for meaning, for sense, for a reason to live is obstructed by the outerworldliness of this very desire itself. The desire for the impossible is not only a desire for the beyond, but also to feel that what it is I am, the road of human becoming I'm on, is not a purely given, static becoming, forcing me along. The question of the impossible is just as much an essential element of my relationship with becoming itself, as it is a question of moving beyond my becoming. But no matter what I attain, every time I feel I have obtained what my longing asked for, I realise this object gained was an illusion and instantaneously my desire shifts to something else. Something more – always more, always better, always different.

Desire is thus the force that shapes, that creates pathways, that makes me traceable. It is closely related to my political life, the life out in the open that is constructed and breakable. "Drives and part-objects are neither stages on a genetic axis nor positions in a deep structure; they are political options for problems, they are entryways and exits, impasses the child lives out politically, in other words, with all the force of this or her desire."[158]

157 Georges Bataille, *Méthode de Méditation*, Vol.5, p.207.
158 Gilles Deleuze and Félix Guattari, *A Thousand Plateaus*, p.13.

Desire is not a lack. "For me, desire does not comprise any lack; neither is it a natural given; it is but one with an assemblage of heterogenous elements which function; it is process, in contrast with structure or genesis; it is affect, as opposed to feeling; it is "*haecceity*" (individuality of a day, a season, a life), as opposed to subjectivity; it is event, as opposed to thing or person."[159] Desire is itself a becoming visible, audible, traceable. It is not a void, although it might be pointing towards or resulting from one.

Attempting to visualise, to name, to hear, to acknowledge this desire for the beyond, facing this impossible, this paradox, leaves me empty. There is nothing else, unbiddable, ungovernable, like a riot in the heart, and nothing to be done, come ruin nor rapture.[160]

Acting out this political longing, this desire that shapes my being, makes me incapable of not living. It is not an animal instinct, but a very human capacity to desire, to desire even in such a way that we destroy that what we have built. I blind myself, I shut out rationality, just in order to obtain a fleeting glimpse of my desire. Yet my desire is never obtainable. There is nothing left but to despair over this fundamental crisis. Whosoever realises this internal paradox, finds herself in despair, in the state of being that leaves everything unhinged, that makes being uncanny, to not-be at home in my own life, my own world, as I always already long for something that is not.

159 Gilles Deleuze, *Desire and Pleasure*, pp. 59-65.
160 John Madden, *Shakespeare in Love*.

ILLUSION

There is no way of reaching the beyond, of thinking the impossible, of even approaching it. There is no real change. If this is all there is to conclude, then what is left for me to do? There is nothing stopping me from fortressing myself, or from ending up depressed and suicidal. Perhaps I should be thankful to always already being thrown into language, into my personal, specific discourse that makes me believe there is meaning and truth. As it is because of these illusions I make for myself, the claims to change and alter reality, to influence the world around me, that actually keep me sane and alive. Without retaining even a mere shimmer of the possibility of change, everything I undertake and everything that is done by others would be doomed to be other instances of once again the same.

I need to acknowledge that radical change cannot be perceived as such, that there are no examples that can confirm the existence of true change. Therefore, I need to face the fact that the existence of radical change relies on mere hope, on an idealism that is basing everything in my own thinking – which itself could very well be flawed and superficial. If thinking itself creates the (im)possibilities for change, who am I fooling when I say that there is only change, to claim that change is everywhere, there for the taking?

But then, to say there is no change, that everything always remains the same, why would that be any different? I am right to question whether this impossibility of change, the impossibility of ever reaching the impossible, is true only for myself, because it is the way I happen to think. Is it me thinking this, does it just happen to be part of my discourse, or is there some truth, reality to it that makes it true for everyone? The question is genuine. Is this my epistemic nonsense, or is this that non-existent, impossible 'Truth' which moves beyond the limits of my own discourse? And why do I find this question so important, this material reflection of my longing for the impossible? What makes this question for the beyond breathe life into everything?

On what basis can I claim a truth that goes beyond my own discourse, and perhaps even beyond the episteme in which I find myself? Does this bring me back to the original impossibility, of not being able to reach for the beyond? Am I merely stuck in my own circle, my own episteme, my own world? Or does it have further implications, does it also mean that my world does not allow for real change? Why then do I keep repeating that same singular oneness, that same mantra, the song which echoes in my ears – that modifications of the real may be possible, but they are illusions when the aim is radical alterity, and the only answer to this impediment is to long for the impossible. The impossible, which includes the unknowable and those things that cannot exist.

Is my longing, my desire to go beyond also annihilating itself at the same time? Is the movement beyond everything that is what I am myself, at the same time also a denial of that same longing? Can I accept that this movement towards the impossible can become superfluous once the impossible is attained? Can I sacrifice this ultimate longing, that which gives life, that which distinguishes animal-humans from human-humans, that which is so utterly dear to me? Or is this denial of myself yet another form of nihilism that is devastating for one's own life and never leads to any particular notion that is more than destruction?

DESPAIR

Considering the limits that confront my thinking and any possibility for original thought, all original thought must be deemed impossible. Language is a force, forcing me into a specific discourse, and in fact my whole thinking is already taking place within this discourse, leaving me doomed to fail from the moment I start to think, to be. Any longing for change, for leaving this plane of existence and radically entering the beyond, for a fundamental change as opposed to a mere modification of the same, is in itself impossible. I repeat myself, which is perhaps the only thing left to do, and the only thing within my reach.

The essence of existentialism is not the opportunity of choosing. It is always already taking place within the desire *for* something. It is the choosing *something*. Something that is not within the realm of the possible, but always already outside it. Yet when I face this essential feature of existential life I am forced to leap into the despair of being trapped inside the box.

Does this mean that I am then always confined to suffering this despair?

> *Suffer bravely, myriads!*
> *Suffer for the better world!*
> *Up above the firmament*
> *A great God will give rewards.*[161]

Being faced with a permanent state in which there is no fundamental change possible does not mean my desire for the beyond has faltered. My desire has even heightened. It creates an urgency: if I cannot reach for this beyond, is there anything left in life to pursue?

161 Schiller, *Ode to Joy*, §5.

I might as well stop being human altogether. This feeling-human is an illusion, if not for the ability to question this beyond. What is left if that is taken away? If that road is blocked forever? It is this desire, and my continuing to accept and embrace this desire for the impossible, that makes me last. It makes me take another step, albeit one that creates yet another distance between me and the beyond, always linking myself to the past and into the future. There is no way of experiencing this moment by itself, not originally; there is always already the frame that binds me. But at the same time, the same moment, I am also still faced with this impossible plight. How can I cope with this dreadful situation, being locked into a world in which I am thrown, unable to move from and to even think outside of? How can I let go of this despair, without simultaneously letting go of who I am?

I might turn to the wise men that have walked the earth before me, unaware as I am of their female counterparts. Kierkegaard explained[162] how despair comes about not when one is faced with the end, with death. Death is a way out, an end to suffering, and can therefore never really be the source of despair. Death should be seen as the absolute moment of the impossible, the state of the beyond that can never be obtained – for once one is dead, one is no longer. Yet it is not our understanding of being mortal, our facing the impossibility of having to die, that leaves us in despair. Despair comes only when the possibility of death is taken away from us. "When death is the greatest danger, one hopes for life; but when one becomes acquainted with an even more dreadful danger, one hopes for death. So, when the danger is so great that death has become one's hope, despair is the disconsolateness of not being able to die."[163]

162 See: Soren Kierkegaard, *Sickness unto Death.*
163 Soren Kierkegaard, *Sickness unto Death*, p.15.

The outlook of not being able to change my position, of being faced with the inevitability of everything that is and will always be, when realising the marginal changes in the form of modification and transformation that one can achieve at the most — I am faced with a most mundane despair. I must face the everything-ness, the multitude that overwhelms as there is no escape. "Everything that is, is too much,"[164] Bataille exclaimed. It is exactly the type of despair Kierkegaard already warned about, which comes about when put in a position in which the possibility is taken away. Once it becomes apparent that we're stuck inside the episteme, the escape out of the present has been forcefully taken away from us. And to realise this takes away this possibility, by being ourselves, by being aware, by becoming attained and attuned to that which always already is. Even if we have no choice except to continue to be present in the present. "A self that has no possibility is in despair..."[165]

I could leave it at that and end my humanity, my life, with saying that the correct method in philosophy would be to say nothing except what can be said, and to pass over in silence over the rest. As some do. Or I could conclude is that there is no change possible. As some do. Or I could look at all change as a *mauvaise foi*, a bad faith that is an illusion I tell myself in order to keep myself occupied to not face the inevitable: everything that is, will always be, whatever we do. As some do.

The most common way to overcome this paradox, would be to forget about this despair, this being forced into a discourse from which there is no real escape. I could choose to become, to be, to exist merely as a Follower of the world in which I find myself. I could become a Consumer who actively chooses from the options that this illusionary world of possibilities offers me.

164 Georges Bataille, *Méthode de Méditation*, p.228.
165 Soren Kierkegaard, *Sickness unto Death*, p.37.

Or I could become entangled with the illusions of revolution, of thinking change, of professing progress. All are desperate measures trying to overcome the essential despair that the desire for the impossible brings us.

But why then am I still thinking, writing, still translating thought, still forcing myself to take up the frame, when it is precisely that which leaves me all alone, devoid of meaning that is real, in a despair that is paradoxically giving life to it all? "Anguish makes reading forbidden (the words separated, something arid and devastating; no more text, each word useless, or else foundering in something that I do not know, drawing me into it with refusal, comprehension as an injustice). To write then, the effect of a negative hallucination, giving nothing to read, nothing to understand."[166] This anxiety, this anguish, this despair makes it impossible, makes it a place not to go, where each word pushes me into the realm of that which presents itself as knowledge, as comprehension, but which is only there to haunt me, to push me into the epistemic depths of reasonableness. It is "the falsity of the traps into which [I] am driven, no less than the reflection of the other in the mirror of words (a mirror that always also reflects the self and its investments in the glaring inadequacy of words and concepts), to an 'I' displaced in the passion of relation to the other."[167]

166 Maurice Blanchot, *The Step Not Beyond*, p.63.
167 Christopher Fynsk, *Last Steps*, p.161.

CONTROL / FOLLOWER

To overcome this despair of the impossible, I can choose to play along with the illusion of obtaining, I can fake the perfect life and the American dream, and do it in such a manner that I am unaware, unconscious, unknowing to the fact that it is an illusion that starts to control my dreams and the initial desire. It is a *mauvaise foi* that binds me to gravity. It is a giving in to the structure in which I find myself, it is becoming a follower of the discourse I find myself in. Something I always already am, even without thinking about it. There is nothing unusual about it, it would be pleasant and comfortable to snuggle in my very own corner of the episteme, wrapping myself in the discourse of my life. I become truly, as part of that crowd which is untruth, I become what has been labelled a herd animal. Why not embrace this curse of the modern individual, becoming the Follower of that what is, the one that traces the being present without any motive that reaches beyond, this being constrained by the discourse in which one finds herself. It is this "ideological 'big Other' (tradition), embodied in its apparatuses (rituals), [that] interpellates individuals, and it is up to the individual to live and act in accordance with the title that makes him what he is."[168]

The follower-me exchanges her humanity for the feeling of control over her own desire. It creates the identity that she finds herself thrown in. Yet follower-me forgets that desire is not something to have or to simply disregard. It is a force that propels, that leaves nothing untouched, that destroys, that creates. Desire cannot be controlled, but can be chosen, actively sought, nourished and embellished. Once I choose to control life, I lose my desire. Once I desire, I lose control.

168 Slavoj Žižek, *Demanding the Impossible*, p.11.

Follower-me feels this need to control herself and the world around her as a way to make sense of reality. When there is no origin, no reason for something to happen that she can know, predict and control, then everything that happens to her, is outside of reason. The feeling of despair starts lurking around the corner. Which is why the follower, despite being unable to grasp the origin of things, will create illusions that make her believe she understands it all, naming it along the way, framing whatever loose ends she might find. This is not done out of spite, it is the only way to value the world and her personal life. When she can control what happens, she can also be responsible and proud of whatever she achieves. She becomes an individual, distinguishable from the others within the group that she herself has labelled as described by her discourse, as 'human', blocking out the Other. Her life becomes valuable. Yet she has lost being, she has undone her being human. As Blanchot describes, "the libertine is thoughtful, self-contained, incapable of being moved by just anything." In her the feeling of control has made her conform to the existing structures of what is supposed, of that what is normal. She is taken over by "[a]pathy [as] the spirit of negation, applied to the man who has chosen to be sovereign."[169]

The voicing of the desire, which is stressed in psychoanalysis,[170] is not the cure of the desire, but it is the attempt of bringing the impossible into the realm of the known.[171] I might be confronted with a feeling of relief, but this is always an illusion, an illusion of control and understanding. Despite all, I remain within the illusion, that despair-avoiding mechanism of the *mauvaise foi*, as long as the surplus, that which cannot be named, and the despair accompanying this unnameable, the impossible, is not embraced simultaneously.

169 Maurice Blanchot, *Lautréamont et Sade*, p.256.
170 See: Jacques Lacan, *The Seminars of Jacques Lacan: Book I: Freud's Papers on Technique 1953–1954*
171 See also: Bruce Fink, *The Lacanian Subject: Between Language and Jouissance.*

This desire for control, this need to be able to create something, includes the idea that this creation of the Self and of reality, can happen *ex nihilum*. In Sartre's existentialism this is taken to an extreme, a person can create herself (*exisistentia*) without relating to a preconceived essence of who one is (*essentia*). The creatio *ex nihilim* is a general attitude present in contemporary life, but it is a characteristic of the Follower. Having passed the historical stadium of essence precedes existence, the Follower creates a frame in which the feeling is encouraged that tells her continuously, every moment, that one is free to create one's self every minute, over and over, starting from nothing. Based in the Cartesian realisation that one thinks, the Follower lets go of everything that comes before that realisation, making the illusion of original thought possible. It is thus that Follower-me sees herself as creating an image that confirms her desires. It is no problem to change my reality, the Follower-me tells herself, as there are only new beginnings that are unrelated to the previous moment.

Yet this acquired freedom is in fact only another form of despair. "To be sure it is tempting to conceive of myself as standing out on the undifferentiated ground of the human by means of the impulse of my freedom, by the choice of my unique possibilities…"[172] But this temptation is not leading us anywhere – why is it that I am still longing to go somewhere, to reach something other than that which is? In the end, I will need "to accept the consequence of modernity, which is radical freedom not only in the good sense, but also in the terrifying sense that we have to decide. It' s totally up to us. This is what Lacan means when he says: 'There is no big Other – *il n'y a pas de grand Autre*.'"[173] The problem lies not in (not) having a choice, but in the idea of being able to choose whatever I want – irrespective of the world in which I find myself.

172 Jean-Paul Sartre, *Being and Nothingness*, p.305.
173 Slavoj Žižek, *Demanding the Impossible*, p.11.

NIHILISM AND/OR RELATIVISM

Although Follower-me starts out from a noble desire, she falls into the illusion of controlling desiring by accepting the discourse and the possible choices it offers. Moving through an existentialist attitude, she falls into a meaninglessness from which there seems to be no return. Even Sartre is not able to find a constructive ground in this groundless world. All he could do, is to choose where to place his next step, to stay on the mountain or to let go and let oneself tumble into the depth that is unknown.[174] But this so-called choosing is the illusion that makes us forget that the mountain itself is already there, it is given, pre-ordained, it is the only choice possible. (Not choosing the mountain is yet another way to confirm the episteme, albeit a negative confirmation.) Existentialism is therefore only a delusion from what is truly happening: Follower-me needs to be a nihilist or a relativist to keep up with the changes she is forced to call upon herself.

Unfortunately, neither nihilism nor relativism offers a satisfactory solution to the problem of facing a necessary illusion that we cannot overcome except in death. Nietzsche's nihilism is either a drowning in despair, or the commitment that I need to re-evaluate values that would liberate me from the clutches of the discourse, the frame that has framed me. Perhaps Nietzsche's *Übermensch* is the only being that has no need for worldly support for the values she embodies. The *Übermensch* is the figure beyond, the impossible being, the voice that speaks from nowhere, without words. But by accepting the *Übermensch*, am I not just plunging in another discourse, deluding myself once more?

174 Jean-Paul Sartre, *Being and Nothingness*, p.509ff.

Relativism; it scares me to even consider it. Although it is anti-realist enough, it refrains from saying even 'there is a fact of the matter as to whether or not P.' It is true that the frame of reality makes it necessary that everything that I take to be this reality, only to be so for me, because of my discourse, my world-view. Even reality is relative.[175] Yet relativeness does not need to end up in relativism. If relativism is the conclusion of my life, if this is what can be reached by being a Follower, then there is nothing authentic, everything is an illusion. Even despair itself would be generated by myself. Solipsism entails everything, there would be nothing true even to myself. I would need to stop being a hu-man-be-ing that is more than the animal-deciding what to be/feel/do/act/think.

Fortunately, the desire for the beyond is larger than all this, and even the Follower-me is still holding on to this essential humanness that makes me long for escape, escaping the framing from which there is no escape. This is impossible, while, as I will need to show still in the pages that follow, it is at the same time the ultimate goal of human life. Relativism is giving up. Nihilism is giving up. I will not give up.

175 Nelson Goodman, *Ways of Worldmaking*, p.20.

CHANGE – CONSUMER

Another way of overcoming the despair of the impossible is to tell myself that change is possible. In fact, as has been said by Heraclitus so many years ago, turned into the colloquial truth as we hear it all around us: I cannot jump in the same river twice.[176] So why this despair for not reaching otherness, the impossible? The only thing to reach, is the other. Standing still would be death, so when there is life at all, I will need to conclude that there is only change.

This kind of change is a way of 'progressive' thinking, focusing on the passage of time as a going forward, developing and changing for the better. It is a response, an unwillingness to accept the status quo and it is the fear that the present meaninglessness is the end of the story. After the death of God, I am continually searching for meaning within the frame I find myself in, within this political and social structure that creates a link of the mundane with the sublime.[177] With the disappearing of the positive substance that links to this realm of the sublime, we fear our existence may never reach any goal. I am there among the people at Nietzsche's market square,[178] laughing at the madman trying to explain to me in definite terms the disappearing of God. But although I am not able to listen, I can feel the anxiety that is becoming present at the square. Yet I do not face this anxiety and I do nothing to search for a way to reach my own hill from which to look at the world – which I still feel is merely another illusion of a beyond. I do not create the world and its values anew, I continue to be on this market square, that economic marketplace where one is exchanged for the other, among and amidst the others that are at once alienating and comforting me. I keep on telling my-

176 'We both step and do not step in the same rivers. We are and are not'. Heraclitus, *Homeric Questions*, p.24.

177 See Giorgio Agamben's project of Homo Sacer: *The Sacrament of Language*, p.29ff.

178 See: Friedrich Nietzsche, *Thus Spoke Zarathustra*.

self that I cannot leave, that this is where life happens. I continue to shop for a meaning of life that makes me feel good, at least for the time being. I have become a Consumer.

Being a Consumer is a continual state of bad faith, an *Uneigentlichkeit* (un-authenticity) that is characteristic of what Heidegger referred to as '*das Man*' (the 'They'). The Consumer-me is so enraptured by the possibilities of this world, that I have told myself that it is precisely my effort to be included in this world is what changes everything. I matter, precisely by being my very own Consumer-me.

My Consumer-me is in a continuous bad faith. Based on the assumption that all human behaviour is the result of a choice, be it conscious or not, there is this image the Consumer-me creates of herself. Consumer-me shops until it finds the ideology that fits, an image it wants to live up to, wants to resemble, and as it goes along life and direct its behaviour, it is always doing this in relation to this representation of herself. There are many ways in which I could do this. Authentically, by which is meant that the I would fully subscribe to this image created by myself. Or in-authentically, for instance out of necessity, unconsciously following whatever I feel is required by my surrounding. This in-authenticity is embraced by the Consumer-me. By placing myself as an object within the world, the Consumer-me loses her ability to choose individually, but instead becomes a robot whose essence is created by the image created by others, the world. The marketplace offers nothing but images that satisfy the longing to choose, but the choices one is presented with are not related to our desires.

This is why Antigone is such an anti-heroine. Never one asks about her state of mind, her longing, her truth. Instead, she is propelled forth by facing this choice, and appearing to actively choose – whereas in reality there is no choice, she is always already destined to act as she did. Don't confuse her decisiveness for grandeur or bravery: she creates the image she was by being exactly the one thing she could be, was allowed to be.

Another instance of a Consumer-illusion-of-change is the stubbornly installed in the contemporary common practise called 'democracy'. The basic idea of democracy is that when all Consumers voice their needs and desires, and when those voices come together, the result will be the greater good. Not only does the Consumer-me think she will achieve a good life for all through democratic processes, but the Consumer-me also uses democracy to satisfy the need to actively choose, to actively create the image of the structure of the world in which she finds herself. The democratic tool is thus extremely powerful as it binds together all Consumers by means of their desire to create. Even if nothing comes of it, if structures and frames and reality continue to be the same.

ILLUSION OF REVOLUTION

It is the Consumers who start revolutions. Revolution is the ultimate idea of change, of altering something in such a way, that a transformation takes place. Consumers want us to see revolution as a breaking of the existing political order, the existing system of thought, the discourse present in the world. And although revolutions are often bloody and many Consumers sacrifice their lives in order to make the change they have in mind happen, revolutions should not be taken as a going beyond, as a fundamental change. Revolution is one more illusion, instigating Consumers to be happy with resembling themselves as and within their choices.

Let us distance ourselves from Immanuel Kant's hailing of the French Revolution, which Žižek was so quick to relate to the Egyptian uprising of February 2011.[179] "The recent Revolution of a people which is rich in spirit, may well either fail or succeed, accumulate misery and atrocity, it nevertheless arouses in the heart of all spectators (who are not themselves caught up in it) a taking of sides according to desires which borders on enthusiasm and which, since its very expression was not without danger, can only have been caused by a moral disposition within the human race."[180] There are many reasons as to why this 'desire bordering on enthusiasm' is a mere illusion that instantly gratifies the observer, someone not even involved, not part of the so-called 'event' of revolution. It is true that consequences do not make for a revolution or event, but there is nothing here that shows *why* exactly we should take this kind of revolution to be a true event, a breaking of the present. As Kant himself said in a text from the very same year, a revolutionary Consumer spirit may overthrow autocratic despotism but could never amount to "a true reform in ways of thinking. Rather, new prejudices will serve as old

179 See for instance: Slavoj Žižek, *Less than Nothing*, p.34.
180 Immanuel Kant, *The Conflict of Faculties*, p.182.

ones to harness the great unthinking mass"[181] of illusion-following Consumers.

Revolution is that moment in which the question 'what is to be done' is answered positively. As Jeremy Fernando puts it: "The moment Lenin set out to answer the question, he set in place a revolution – a continual circle which ends up exactly where it begins – which ensured the end to any possibilities."[182] The end to any possibilities of being open to the impossible, that is.

A revolution may clean out the marketplace of all the rubble and images of reality that are sold there. The revolutionary Consumer-me feels like she releases the wrath of Christ, kicking out the swindlers from the house of God, that all-encompassing image of the Other. Yet what the Consumer-me does not understand, is that the same house remains, the world is not changed, new thoughts have not emerged through this emptying. The flavour might be different, the sounds may appear changed, yet the fact that it is still *products* sold on the *marketplace*, makes this an illusion of change. Every revolution that busies itself with a taking down, instead of a construction of something that is impossible, something that is unrelated to all the structures of 'what is', is a failed revolution. It is even a false revolution, an illusion that occupies the mind of the Consumer-me and fights off despair, albeit illusionary and only a momentary respite.

There are so many examples of this type of illusion, the illusion of change, of revolution. They are only successful in one respect: they instil the Consumers with a feeling of ability, of being able to create anew. Yet what they forget, is that they mix two notions of revolution, "they're constantly confusing two different things, the way revolutions turn out historically and people's revolutionary becoming. These relate to two different sets of people. Men's only hope lies in a revolutionary becoming: the only way of casting off their shame

181 Immanuel Kant, *An Answer to the Question: What is Enlightenment.*
182 Jeremy Fernando, *Reading Blindly*, p.62.

or responding to what is intolerable."[183] For whenever true Becoming takes place, the putting into place of something truly new, the attainment of the impossible, that surely would honour the need to be called revolution. Just not in the illusionary historical, political sense the notion 'revolution' is used nowadays.

At most, revolutions are the becoming conscious of what was always already there...[184]

183 Gilles Deleuze, *Negotiations*, p.171.
184 Michel Foucault, *Archaeology of Knowledge*, p.23.

ILLUSION OF THINKING CHANGE

Am I just pretending to be searching for something which is original, by once again repeating that which has been said before? Perhaps that is the only thing left for me to do, to repeat always the primary instance of that event that was original, that was true.

There is nothing original to claiming that there is no fundamental change possible. It is the framing, the limitedness of the human intellect that makes change itself impossible. This is nothing new, I only need to follow the reasoning of Immanuel Kant to see how this is true. Kant systematically approached the position of human rationality in connection with the sensible world I inhabit. By doing so, Kant created a – what he called Copernican – revolution in human history and thinking. One more revolution that is illusionary except for a semantic meaning that brings to the present that reality which we already inhabit...

For Kant, the human being was no longer a part of the world in the way she had been thus far, an inhabitant in a strange conjuncture of beings that were there and she had to make sense of. It is no wonder that for Foucault, Kant is the changing point in history, the beginning of modernity.[185] Instead, human-being became the centre of the universe. By deciding and interpreting the world, she not only created understanding, but created the world as well. By showing that there is nothing empirically given in the world in as far as it is not already theoretically pre-structured by human-being, Kant opened the way for modernity, the way for doubt and anxiety to become the basis of reality itself. Instead of describing an ideology to recapture all the forms of representation, "Kantian critique questions representation on the basis of its rightful limits."[186]

185 See: Michel Foucault, *The Order of Things*.
186 Michel Foucault, *The Order of Things*, p.242.

It questions "all that is the source and origin of representation" and Foucault is correct to say that this created "the question of what it means for thought to have a history."[187]

This Kantian approach is another way of saying that any change I observe in the world is because *I* observe it. And, more importantly, because I can *think* it. Any change, any object or state that I observe as being in the world is not a completely empirical given, it is something that has been influenced by the way I can conceive of things. Not only discourses frame me, the schematics of reason itself limits and constructs my perception. This makes it a difficult question as to whether there can be any change *an sich,* as it lies beyond the categories of thought. According to Immanuel Kant there is no change at all, as change is a category of human thinking, it is not *of* the world, but only comes about from within my own capacity to think. There is therefore no change *an sich*, even when there is a perception or experience of change in the reality we find ourselves in.

What does this mean for me, desiring change and longing for a beyond? Concluding that there is no change *an sich* is not very informative in itself. (Except for noting that perhaps Wittgenstein was right all along?) It does show, however, the importance of knowing the limits of my own thinking. And more important, it shows the necessity of my own thinking. Heidegger referred to this when he took up his major project of the thinking again of *being*: the fact that one person may have succeeded in systematically thinking *being*, does not mean that everything and even *being* itself has been properly and completely thought. (Despite what Hegel may have meant, when he decided history had ended because he had thought it.) We all have to think everything all over again, every person again. This is a direct consequence of the Kantian understanding, that it is the human intellect that shapes my own understanding and experience, down to the most basic level of experience. Phenomenology, and

187 Michel Foucault, *The Order of Things*, p.219-20.

especially the hermeneutics developed by Hans-Georg Gadamer, takes this exertion quite seriously,[188] trying to let go of all the over-arching stories, truths that are assumed without relying on one's own relationship to it. The thing itself cannot be trusted, the grounding of being can only be constituted by tracing everything myself, the relationship of the I with the thing.

In this sense, change is in the eye of the beholder. It is conceived and promulgated by the one who thinks it. So, thinking change is the illusion of reason itself: it is nothing but a confirmation of the frame I am myself. But this does not lead to enlighten my basic desire, my longing to think the impossible and thereby letting the beyond fundamentally change the world. It does show me that to understand change in the world, I need to account for the manner in which I understand this world and how the nature of our thinking limits the possibilities of change in this world. But tracing the frame will not un-frame it.

I dance in front of the mirror that shows me changing images, that I see, and instead of breaking the glass, I am content with what the mirror shows me, the light that reflects gives me a myriad of changing images that are nothing but a confirmation of what already was. I look in the mirror, and I see what I already was. The illusion of the frame confirms my longing, but doesn't bring me one step closer to what the mirror cannot show me.

And there I am, back at the original despair for which no illusion seems strong enough. There is no revolution: there is nothing but the illusion of change.

188 See for instance: Hans-Georg Gadamer, *Philosophical Hermeneutics*.

ILLUSION OF PROGRESS

Faced with the non-being of change, the eternal recurrence of that what is, of me thinking the world and everything in it, in order to accept this, there is one more illusion that will need to make way — the illusion of progress.

Everything in contemporary life seems to be focussed on going forward, moving on, looking ahead. Where does this linear thinking come from, this outlook of time as an addition instead of a negation? Is this whole of modern thinking, the enlightenment and all those other terms that create an idea of a growth, a facade, an illusion to keep me occupied with framing myself, in this never-changing world of despair?

"History is nothing but believing in meaning, believe the lie."[189] Or as Lyotard explains to us, "we can see that historical periodization belongs to an obsession that is characteristic of modernity. Periodization is a way of placing events in a diachrony, and diachrony is ruled by the principle of revolution."[190] But I am always already thinking it, within it, history. History, historical reality is a thought. Even if I listen to what Ricoeur has to say in his exploration of approaching historical reality, this leaves me on the side of the possible.

If there is no change, is there then only the Same? When the possible thoughts are always the same but merely thought in different times, don't I just leave out the fact that there is a difference, even though it might be insignificant and still limited to the same world that is? When I take the historical reality as the idea of the same, historical traces are merely re-enactments of the past. "To introduce oneself through thought into an action in order to discern in it the thought of its agent is precisely to re-think in one's own mind

189 Friedrich Nietzsche, *Götzen-Dämmerung*, p.68.
190 Jean-François Lyotard, *The Inhuman*, p.25.

what was once thought."[191] But this is not leading anywhere, I am still faced with the limits of my world, and my desire to transcend it. History, or the thought of time, is just obscuring the boundaries, trying to trick me into thinking I can effectively re-think, whereas looking at history as a repeating of the same could never be done except when we would assume that there is something like "non-exchangeable and non-substitutable singularities."[192] But this type of repetition is as un-historic as can be, and therefore a possible way out of the possible. And especially that is what historical thinking obscures.

So how should I understand time? Time as without historical reality, without progress, without direction? Time can mean many things. But perhaps I am interested only in experienced time. In itself, of course, is another discursive reality, another framing of what is. It is only once more describing something that makes me hope to break free from the given, whereas it is only a confirmation of that which binds me. Time is not just a concept for Kant: time is something in which I am enclosed, that I can in no way try to escape. Even when the clock stops ticking, I cannot deny that time passes. This is how I experience time. This experienced time has nothing to do with clocks. Instead, it has everything to do with the present. The moment in which I fall, in which I become, in which I am trapped to be. (Even language is framed as a time, the rhythm of speaking that moves me, propels me and lets me breathBergson already explained how the present time is not just a moment that will become past the next moment. The present is already the past, and it is this thick present that we experience. But isn't the same true for the future? Isn't the future already linked to my present, isn't my present gaze the same as the one that will look into the next moment? It is our linear experience and our linear positing of time that makes both past and future limited to the present present.

191 Paul Ricoeur, *The Reality of the Historical Past*, p.7-8.
192 Gilles Deleuze, *Difference and Repetition*, p.1.

And as such, the idea of progress is nothing but an illusion. As Benjamin mentions of the angel of history, it drives him "irresistibly into the future, to which his back is turned, while the rubble-heap before him grows sky-high."[193]

193 Walter Benjamin, *On the Concept of History*, IX.

ACCEPTANCE

This desire for the unframing of the frame, the going beyond, the non-acceptance of reality as it is, brings me to a becoming beyond the Follower and the Consumer. Precisely because the desire for change is a fundamental illusion, we need to look ahead. Ahead, in a non-judgmental, non-linguistic, non-historical, non-sense. Any term that already makes sense by itself, from itself, will limit the fulfilment my impossible desire, which is already the case. So why am I still forcing it into language, why am I dwelling on it?

Perhaps my every-day solution to facing of the impossible is itself the *mauvaise foi*, the illusion of change, which is helpful enough to get me through to the next moment, the next illusion, the next deluded choice, that makes up every-day life.

But at the moment I am touched by that radical other that is the beyond, my humanity, human-ness, beyond animal-ness, comes to the surface, and I am again reminded that there is something I truly long for, namely this fundamental radical other, which is the impossible, the beyond, which is the change that is never already there. How can there be this longing when it doesn't come from somewhere, when all the roads are already closed off?

This will need to be explored, and will be explored in the next chapter, once this general pause is done, once my voice of desire has again subsided.

But this movement is never to be seen as an escape, the despair will continue and will continue to force itself onto the framed self, as it points at that which our desire masks.

Despite this control, the original desire remains unfulfilled. Is it the question, the naming, the putting the desire into language, that is already the fulfilling of the desire that always remains unfulfilled? "Rene Char says: *"The poem is the realized love of desire that has remained desire."*""[194]

Do I only desire? Is becoming more than longing?

It's time to move into the mystical realm of the impossible. Every step I take to overcome the despair of the impossibility of attaining the impossible, is a move that closes off the opportunity. Time is of the essence, the despair I face can overtake me any moment and leave me meaningless behind, devoid of truth and sense, along a road that is not even my own.

194 Maurice Blanchot, *The Infinite Conversation*, p.40.

PART III

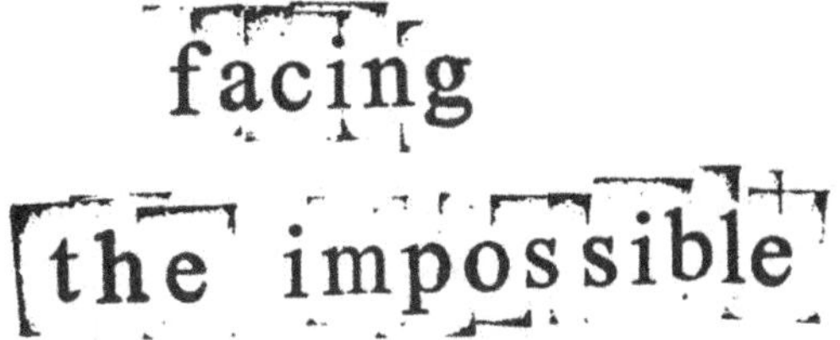

After having framed our thinking, and dealt with the ensuing despair, it is time. Time to acknowledge our desire for the impossible. And time to face the fact that what emerges is at best a hope, a facing of what will always remain other.

INTRODUCTION

> "Simply put, there will be two types of [philosophy]. One, which is infrascientific and nonsensical because it attempts to bend non-thought by force into the theoretical proposition, is the philosophical sickness proper. The other, suprascientific, silently affirms non-thought as a 'touching' of the real. It is the authentic 'philosophy', which is a conquest of antiphilosophy."
> ~ Alain Badiou, Wittgenstein's Antiphilosophy

There is a human desire towards the impossible, and the untenability of this desire leads to despair over the impending result of failure. We cannot change the way in which we think, in which we perceive reality and the possible. We are framed by the very desire that tries to un-frame to reach the beyond.

What would happen when tracing our desire for the impossible would stop here? If all change is illusionary – not merely the change we can observe or experience, but every change that can be imagined and every change that could ever be imagined – then we are to find a way to be content with the illusions with which we have surrounded ourselves. Relativism and nihilism would never be adequately silenced. We could simply continue our lives, creating illusionary structures as we have done for such a long time already. Nothing would change. And perhaps we could at some level even be happy with that *status quo*.

But is a Nietzschean project of re-evaluation of values, of constructing something irrespective of its previous being, always impossible? The desire for the impossible, and the ultimate desire for its consequence in the form of fundamental change, does not diminish due to its impossibility. As a matter of fact, its sheer impossibility makes it a worthy project in the first place. Worthy, as in life-giving, meaningful, human. Philosophy's quest for the impossible would only be reinforced by this conclusion of impossibility. Our search for real change, for a beyond that is human, has in some respects only just started. So far, we've only been clearing our throats, tracing, working our way forward between the rubble of possibilities.

It is time to turn to what is the main concern here. Not because we have the time on our side – that folly of youth! – but precisely because there is no time to lose. Every moment spent in a reading that distracts, in listening to people that are Followers or Consumers, listening to our fears and feelings of inadequacy, makes us to be more and more trapped inside the world of the possible. Being true to our desire, our goal is not just a pointing, a showing of the cards, a taking apart of this question of the impossible, of showing the limits of the world. No, by all that is beyond! We aim at a construction of something valuable beyond the frame that creates truth and meaning: a conception of change that is not limited by its contemporary episteme. And aiming thus, we are fundamentally preconditioned to fail — and do we reach exactly what is human?

How nice would it be to have an example of the beyond. To have an instance, even if it is only a moment, in which our desire is fulfilled. To sing a song, write a symphony, to draw, paint. Would they fulfil the desire, even though they will not move beyond what is already possible? To make someone – myself – *experience* the beyond, to do away with all these words that are only distracting. That don't clear the way, but are only describing and pointing out the obstacles that together form everything that distracts from this 'way'. The way, only named as such because we are unable to walk it, and this inability, the thought of being unable, is one of the main obstacles. The not-walking itself is the inability. There is no thing-in-itself, there is no reality, no world, no way outside of the epistemic constructions, contraptions.

And this is not where it ends, this despair is only the beginning. We are philosophers, tracing our steps annoyingly until all our understanding bursts. We are repeating the road Cioran already prescribed, even though we are (also) women… "There are men who started in the world of abstract forms and ended in absolute confusion. Therefore, they can only philosophize poetically. In the state of absolute confusion, only the delight and torments of madness still matter."[195]

195 Emil Cioran, *The Heights of Despair*, p.77.

POSSIBLE IMPOSSIBLE, THE END OF A DICHOTOMY?

"A new type of thinking is essential if mankind is to survive and move toward higher levels..."
~ Albert Einstein, *New York Times*

Facing the impossible starts with a forgetting. Forgetting the dichotomy between the possible and the impossible is the first step to take. A forgetting while never leaving it out of sight. A hearing without listening. Because listening is already a framing, a making sense. It is the first step on the path leading no-where, to that place that is un-place-able as it does not stand in relation to anything we know, think, do, see, hear, live. But is it then simply the Hegelian *Aufhebung* that we're after here? "Within the finite order, we cannot experience or see that the goal is truly achieved. The accomplishment of the infinite goal resides only in overcoming the illusion that this goal is not yet achieved."[196]

Wait, let us go back. What was this possible again? Let us retrieve Blanchot from the depths of the archive that surrounds us wherever we go. The possible is precisely the world that is, that always already is, *il y a*, *das Man*. That empty frame that encompasses not only everything that is real and can be real, but itself also is this possibility, this power to be real. This frame of the possible is always already empowering and overpowering us, as "our relations in the world and with the world are always, finally, relations of power *[puissance]*, insofar as power is latent in possibility."[197] Power – but what is power, power over something or power with something?[198] That limit of language, to distinguish or not, between *Kraft* and *Macht* – to exercise power as an ability (*Kraft*), or to over-power (*Macht*).

196 G.W.F. Hegel, *Die Logik*, p.384.
197 Maurice Blanchot, *The Infinite Conversation*, p.42.
198 See: Michael Karlberg, *Beyond the Culture of Contest*.

Are we then left with only the option to trace the etymology, to see what is meant? *Puissance*, from the Old French *poier*, to be able.[199] Is this whole enterprise a trick: is it us who see the power of the discourse, the epistemic reality as a power over us, within which we are trapped? And is it even a power as a means to do something, an ability? How can something that is limiting us, that exercises power over us, be at the same time the very ability that enables us to act? Or is what we can do precisely the possible that we need to move away from? Where do we find what is necessary to cross the threshold?

We are faced with a paradox. Whenever we ask for the unknown, the impossible, we are faced with the force of language to violate the threshold towards the unknown. "What is to be known—the unknown—must surrender to the known. But then comes this apparently innocent question: might there not exist relations, that is to say a language, escaping this movement of force through which the world does not cease to accomplish itself? In this case, such relations, such a language, would also escape possibility."[200] Innocent enough, but despairingly so. It puts us right in the depth of our relational being which is always in touch with the possible itself. Is there a power we can search for that is the possible and the ability to transcend that very possible, itself, at the same time?

It is important to note that to transcend does not mean to become on another plane. There is only the world. Already. Always. We cannot reach outside of this world and go into a different sphere to escape 'world'. If we could, that would mean that 'other' sphere would already be the present, and therefore be already a part of the world itself, all over again. Which is why there is only the moment itself, not the understanding or the realisation of the transcendent moment. There is only the act, which is the religious act. But there is no history of acts. And therefore, no dogma, no strict method of

199 Online Etymology Dictionary, http://www.etyonline.com.
200 Maurice Blanchot, *The Infinite Conversation*, p.43.

reaching the unreachable, of that which remains always impossible.

We need to find a way in which the 'impossible' is no longer related to the possible, which would otherwise frame and limit any action we might take. "This is why Lacan's formula for overcoming an ideological impossibility is not 'everything is possible', but 'the impossible happens.' The Lacanian impossible-real is not an *a priori* limitation, which needs to be realistically taken into account, but the domain of action. An act is more than an intervention into the domain of the possible – an act changes the very coordinates of what is possible and thus retroactively creates its own conditions of possibility,"[201] So, that what is done, has been done, can only be done, when seen afterwards, when judged, when considered, when taken in, can only come to us from within the episteme, is always already within the realm of the possible exactly in as much as it is possible. But more importantly, it is the act itself that has the ability to create the very conditions, the reasons of existence, the traces and relation to the possible.

It is this act, this movement, this reaching that is at stake and which we need to recover from the depths of our despairing self. We need to be realists and request the impossible, following that slogan from the 1960s in France. A slogan that led nowhere while at the same time being the transcendence itself. A slogan that was drenched in illusion, as it allowed for a repetition of the same within the structure of what is.

Perhaps we should refrain from speaking the every-day-language that unites us in our worldly frames, and continue mumbling an un-precise paradox that leaves everything in the neutral between the possible and the impossible. Because when the impossible becomes merely one more type of possible that is only distanced in and through time, we have lost ourselves in Consumerism… Or, as Žižek

201 Slavoj Žižek, *Demanding the Impossible*, p.143.

explains it: "What is impossible? Our answer should be a paradox which turns around the one with which I began: *soyons realistes, demandons l'impossible.* The only realist option is to do what appears impossible within this system. This is how the impossible becomes possible."[202]

Or, re-voicing what Kierkegaard has already told us: "Although thinkers say that actuality is the annihilated possibility, yet this is not entirely true; it is the fulfilled, the effective possibility."[203] The impossible must in this sense remain un-actual, the arrival of the impossible must remain beyond anything that can be thought. Whenever it becomes actual, it is fulfilled possibility. Or, according to Derrida, the truly impossible must be "un-predictable, an event worthy of this name… The event must announce itself as im-possible… An event or an invention are only possible as im-possible".[204] "If only what is already possible, that is, expected and anticipated, happens, this is not an event. The event is possible only when come from the impossible. It happens (*arrive*) *as* the advent of the impossible."[205] And this arriving is what Derrida calls ethics, and the beginning of that which is human.[206] But let's go back once more. Trace the untraceable, to not mistakenly take the paths that trap us to being only one more possibility.

The impossible cannot be approached through the possible. We need something that is neither. Which is not a third category beyond the dichotomy of the possible-impossible. We need to forget this distinction altogether. Forgetting, not by incorporating it into a new discourse that repeats the very same distinctions. We need an un-Hegelian *Aufhebung* that does not destroy the possible, nor create a new possibility.

202 Slavoj Žižek, *Demanding the Impossible*, p.144.
203 Soren Kierkegaard, *Sickness unto Death*, p.12.
204 Jacques Derrida, *Voyous*, p.198.
205 Jacques Derrida, *Papier Machine*, p.285.
206 François Raffould, *The Origins of Responsibility*, p.301.

We need the feminine analysis that is creativity, "out of silence – as an act of creativity, of invention, can transform the unexpected into a new psychic possibility."[207]

The impossible doesn't present itself *as* impossible, because that would already relate it to whatever it already is, namely: not. "Similarly, the event cannot appear to be an event, when it appears, unless it is already repeatable in its very uniqueness. It is very difficult to grasp this idea of uniqueness as immediately iterable, of singularity as immediately engaged in substitution, as Levinas would say. Substitution is not simply the replacement of a replaceable uniqueness: substitution replaces the irreplaceable. The fact that, right away, from the very outset of saying or the first appearance of the event, there is iterability and return in absolute uniqueness and utter singularity, means that the arrival of the arrivant—or the coming of the inaugural event—can only be greeted as a return, a coming back, a spectral revenance."[208] The impossible is therefore always a non-actual event. The event remains impossible, until it emerges into reality: "... the possibility of the event could only be conceived of during its actualization."[209] And after this realisation, whenever we search for it again, it cannot be that what just was. The impossible, when realised, is afterwards immediately, instantly, repetitive, momentarily fallen outside of the depth, into being the unrealisable, unactualisable realm of the impossible.

---

207 Anne Dufourmantelle, *Accueillir l'inespéré.*
208 Jacques Derrida, *A Certain Impossible Possibility*, p. 452.
209 Jeremy Fernando, *Reading Blindly*, p.74.

> "One cannot limit itself to it because the neutral cannot be represented, cannot be symbolized or even signified; moreover it is everywhere, inasmuch as it is borne by the indefinite indifference of the entire narrative..."
> ~ Maurice Blanchot, *The Infinite Conversation*

There is thus something that is neither possible nor impossible, which refers, points, embraces that which is beyond the dichotomy, beyond the distinction that makes everything possible-impossible. The Neutral, the neuter – belonging to neither, as Blanchot tells us:

> what belongs to the neuter is not a third gender opposed to the other two and constituting for reason a determined class of existents or beings. The neuter is that which cannot be assigned to any genre whatsoever: the non-general, the non-generic, as well as the non-particular. It refuses to belong to the category of subject as much as it does to that of object. And this does not simply mean that it is still undetermined and as though hesitating between the two, but rather that the neuter supposes another relation depending neither on objective conditions nor on subjective dispositions.[210]

Overcoming the dichotomy of possible-impossible is thus "a moment of experience capable of undoing all dialectics."[211] Does this make it clear, how and what this experience is like? Can we fathom that which lies beyond the construction of language that frames our very self? "The neuter, the neutral: What are we to understand by this word? — 'Perhaps there is nothing in it to be understood.'"[212] It is the 'perhaps', the 'maybe' that is the answer to the question that cannot be posed. This letting go of demarcations that make sense

210 Maurice Blanchot, *The Infinite Conversation*, p.299.
211 Maurice Blanchot, *The Infinite Conversation*, p.300.
212 Maurice Blanchot, *The Infinite Conversation*, p.303.

of the world that we are always already in, leaves us destitute, alone amidst the rubble of the failed attempt to break the world.

Whatever way we approach, advance, draw near, set about to attempt, to try to seek a way in which to word, to utter, to mouth the original beyond... We never attain it. It is always reached for again and again, until it is actualised and the process starts from the beginning, which is no beginning. "Thus we can begin to surmise that 'impossibility'—that which escapes, without there being any means of escaping it—would be not the privilege of some exceptional experience, but behind each one and as though its other dimension."[213] Mark the 'as though'. Without it, we would plunge into the depths of yet another totalitarian discourse that frames the impossible as possible once again. Blanchot describes three traits of the impossible:

> the present that does not pass, while being only passage; that which cannot be let go of, while offering nothing to hold onto; the too-present to which access is denied because it is always closer than any approach, reversing itself to become absence and thus being the too-present that does not present itself, yet without leaving anything in which one might absent oneself from it...[214]

The impossible *is*, while it is *not*, "without ceasing to be radically different."[215] As such, the impossible is the "mystical limit of the most rational discourse in the world."[216] In and of the world. The possible which through its transcendence ever more becomes, reinforced, applied to an ever-expanding realm of meaning. It creates itself. This call for the impossible remains, even as the possible is ever increasing and expanding as we try to escape it, leaving us both within and outside of the world. We reach for this moving beyond that is not beyond. Perhaps. Maybe. Leaving a gap between everything.

213 Maurice Blanchot, *The Infinite Conversation*, p. 45.
214 Maurice Blanchot, *The Infinite Conversation*, p. 46.
215 Maurice Blanchot, *The Infinite Conversation*, p. 46.
216 Jacques Lacan, *Ecrits*, p.124.

THE APORIA, THE PERHAPS/MAYBE

> "Finally, (...) *aporia*, the impossible, the antinomy, or the contradiction, is a non-passage because its elementary milieu does not allow for something that could be called passage, step, walk, gait, displacement, or replacement, a kinesis in general. There is no more path (*odos, methodos, Weg,* or *Holzweg*). The impasse itself would be impossible."
> ~ Jacques Derrida, *Aporias*

Nietzsche calls for "the philosophers of the dangerous 'perhaps' in every sense."[217] And although often his words are taken as a play of words, a metaphor, there is a wisdom to it when he prefaces his book *Beyond Good and Evil* by supposing truth is a woman – a beyond-dogmatism, a beyond-understanding. A place, a being, that does not adhere to the dogmas inherent in the male-oriented domain called philosophy. Whilst knowing full well that the female is not a counterpart to that which is human — she is just as human as the male, she is not different in reality. Yet she is a break in the long line of male thinkers.[218] She is the object of longing which always creates the distance which can only be overcome by becoming the same. At which point, the impossibility she harbours is lost, has become possible, and leaves the realm of the unapproachable. And from then on, we could even doubt she was ever impossible to begin with. Once something is thinkable, approachable, understandable, it can never be seen or thought of as impossible.

217 Friedrich Nietzsche, *Beyond Good and Evil*, section 2, p.34.
218 See: Genevieve Lloyd, *The Man of Reason*.

The impossible is after all a passageway that cannot be passed. An *aporia*. A- without, *-poros* passage. The *aporia* is the attitude that is the beginning of philosophy, as the Greeks already addressed.[219] It is not to provide answers that lead you through a passageway of learning, as it is not a form of sophistry. It is the acceptance of the not-knowing, the acceptance of the fundamental beyond that can never be grasped, while at the same time instilling you with a drive to continue to reach for it. The *aporia* is the passageway that crumbles once you approach the threshold, once you catch the first glimpse of its existence. It is a road necessarily closed off, as it limits and frames the possible, as it makes reality real and approachable.

The impossible is also essentially human, that human being of being *pantaporos aporos*, having many ways open to her while at the same moment having no way out. Heidegger explains:

> *poros* means: passage through… transition to… path. Everywhere man makes himself a path; he ventures into all realms of the present, of the overpowering power, and in doing so, he is flung out of all paths. Herein is disclosed the entire strangeness of this strangest of all creatures: not only that he tries the essence in the whole of its strangeness, not only that in so doing he *is* a violent one striving beyond his familiar sphere. No, beyond all this he becomes the strangest of all beings because, without issue on all paths, he is cast out of every relation to the familiar and befallen by *ate*, ruin, catastrophe.[220]

219 See: Plato, *Meno*, 84a-c.
220 Martin Heidegger, *Introduction to Metaphysics*, p.150-151.

THE MYSTICAL

> "To anyone who does actually consent to directing his attention and love beyond the world, towards the reality that exists outside the reach of all human faculties, it is given to succeed in doing so. In that case, sooner or later, there descends upon him a part of the good, which shines through him upon all that surrounds him."
> ~ Simone Weil, *Draft for a Statement of Human Obligation*

Looking for the impossible, knowing how it is unreachable and female and essentially human, we find ourselves deeply in the realm of the mystical. The passageway which cannot be traversed is symbolised by the Tree of Extremity, which marks the end of the road, the end of the seventh heaven according to Islamic traditions.[221] And at the same time it marks the beginning of Revelation of that which is.[222] That which lies beyond is not for the human eye, only available for that which is beyond human, Muhammad himself: "[w]e acknowledge that for him [Muhammad] is what lies beyond that which our knowledge cannot attain."[223] It is the limit, the beyond, the place ultimately known as Paradise. That state which is neither heaven nor the world, which once reached cannot be unseen, undone. And it is this reaching that is the goal, the attainment of the Sephirot.

We can even make another passage and tracing into time. Into our human becoming, into the creation of our world. Consider the Greek Gods, for whom name and being were still one. Where each and everyone knew its place and meaning according to an intricate system of belonging. We can see in this world of the Gods a coming together, a being bound together in the creation of offspring, of Penia, poverty, and Poros, the passageway, the Plentiful. They combined

221 As-Sa`di, *Tafsir*, p.819.
222 See: Stephen Lampden, *Encyclopedia*.
223 `Abd al-Karīm al-Jīlī (d. c. 832/1428), 'On the Sidrat al-Muntahā' in sect. 49 of the *al-Insān al-kāmil* (vol.2 pp.12-13) .

their strength and ability to produce Love, into their God-child Eros. As Sarah Kofman remarks, from a historical etymological insightfulness, "the true, philosophical *aporia*, or Penia, is always fertile; in her all opposites are placed under erasure; she is neither masculine nor feminine, neither rich nor poor...neither resourceful nor without resources. This is why *Aporia*, which breaks with the logic of identity, and which pertains to the logic of the intermediary, is an untranslatable term."[224] It is untranslatable precisely because the relation of it to whatever other, other term, other meaning, other being, would mean one is already taking the *aporia*, the place without passage, as a possibility, as an entity that is already there to be translated. Which is why the *aporia* belongs to poverty, to the realm of the perhaps, never constituting reality, but only a perhaps-possible, perhaps-impossible.

Let us call to mind what Derrida has already said as it shows us a truth that is not limited to the discourse we find ourselves in:

> This promising aporia takes the form of the possible-impossible, what Nietzsche called the 'maybe.' Nietzsche writes somewhere that what will be expected from philosophers in the future is an investigation of this 'maybe' that classical philosophers always resisted. And this 'maybe' is not simply an empirical modality: there are some terrible pages in Hegel on the 'maybe' and on those who explore the 'maybe' and whom he regards as empiricists. Nietzsche tries to conceive of a modality of 'maybe' that would not be merely empirical. What I said of the possible-impossible is this 'maybe.' There 'may be' giving, if there is any; if there is, we shouldn't be able to speak of it, to be sure of it. Forgiveness 'may be,' the event 'may be.' In other words, this category of 'maybe,' between the possible and the impossible, belongs to the same configuration as that of the symptom or the secret. The difficulty is in adapting a consequent, theoretical discourse to modalities that seem to constitute so many chal-

224 Sarah Kofman, *Beyond Aporia?* p.27.

> lenges to knowledge and theory. The symptom, the 'maybe,' the possible-impossible, the unique as substitutable, singularity as reiterable, all seem to be nondialectizable contradictions; the difficulty is to find a discourse, that is not simply impressionistic or lacking in rigor, for structures that constitute so many challenges to traditional logic. Have I answered your question? 'Maybe.'[225]

Or are we even misguidedly transgressing the limits, should we not label this aporia-impossible-maybe-perhaps-event as such? Are we to be left in the confused state of doubt that comes over us once we try to overcome it, while enforcing both the possible and the impossible? Are we to approach this matter of overcoming the dichotomy of the possible-impossible, as a manner of looking for what Blanchot referred to as the 'improbable'. Or, are we to question this need to label, to define, to circumscribe? Why now this word 'improbable'? "What does such a word seek to tell us? Were there a meeting point between possibility and impossibility, the improbable would be this point."[226] Yet there is no such meeting point.

Considering the world and the frames it enforces upon us, the power it has over us, it is only this point of improbability that can be considered as *existing* outside of this powering-over us. Existence only has itself as a ground, is not due to a coming into being according to epistemic rules and regulations. It merely is. Blanchot adds: "I dedicate this book to the improbable, that is to say, to what is. To a spirit of vigil. To the negative theologies. To a poetry longed for, of rains, of waiting and of wind. To a great realism that aggravates instead of resolving, that designates the obscure, that takes clarity for clouds that can always be parted. That has concern for a clarity high and impracticable."[227]

225 Jacques Derrida, *A Certain Impossible Possibility*, p.457-458.
226 Maurice Blanchot, *The Infinite Conversation*, p.41.
227 Maurice Blanchot, *The Infinite Conversation*, p.41.

Returning to what this impossible is, it is "perhaps precisely the measure of the other, of the other as other, and no longer ordered according to the clarity of that which adapts it to the same."[228] Maybe, perhaps, I can only approach the impossible by always referring to the other, not committing myself either way, neither by uttering my own thoughts – as they are always already pre-structured and limited by what is – nor by praising the other, as the other is merely another who is trapped in his own way, world. Once we accept that 'what is', the epistemic reality of the world, we come to the Lote Tree that stands at the end and marks the beginning. We refer to it, accept it as a sign not of itself, nor of that which is beyond, we mark it as the *aporia*, the passageway that is not, that cannot be and never will be there.

Let it be certain that here we don't refer to the *aporia* in some kind of analytical sense as described by Nicholas Rescher. An aporia is precisely not what Rescher defines it as: "any cognitive situation in which the threat of inconsistency confronts us."[229] The impossibility cannot confront us: it is beyond; and although we are looking for a way to approach the dread that follows from it, the very idea that this is a cognitive situation, shows that the one who thinks it is not thinking, living, experiencing the original *aporia* itself. *Aporia*, the impossible in-between, the neither/nor. "As though the exercise of absolute power were required, therefore, in order to encounter the limit of this power, no longer solely in its negative form, but as the strange affirmation that escapes being and the negation of being."[230] It is an act, a repetition of the same to find the original element of the singular, repeating the invisible-beyond, because the passed event, the past repetition has become actual and is thereby lost in the structure of the already-present.

228 Maurice Blanchot, *The Infinite Conversation*, p.43-44.
229 Nicholas Rescher, *Aporetics: Rational Deliberation in the Face of Inconsistency*, p.1.
230 Maurice Blanchot, *The Infinite Conversation*, p.184.

PRINCIPLE OF FAILURE

"… the story this world first told itself as it became the modern world."
~ David Berlinski, *A Tour of the Calculus*

The question we've been facing, and are still facing, and probably are always going to be facing, is labouring towards a thinking on the beyond, of how this beyond can or cannot relate to the discourse we inhabit, how it can influence (or: change) the world we find ourselves thrown into. If we would go scientific all of a sudden, or analytic if you prefer, we could simply say that we need to delineate some basic features in order to enable fundamental change. A successful theory is often measured by its effectiveness, its clarity and its applicability. From that perspective, aiming for effectiveness, the manner in which we have been facing our original question, our primordial desire and the resulting despair, would lead us to believe that in order to be successful, in order to reach the beyond, we would need to deliver this beyond to the clutches of the discourse we are embellishing by using language. Yet that is precisely what we have set out not to do, as it would mean we would lose everything that is desirable. It would mean a betrayal of that what is beyond. Whenever we succeed, make feasible, practical, effective, useful, approachable – we have failed. Therefore it is failure that we need to accept. But not a failure that is a negative, as a state of depression, one that measures itself against a success. Nor a failure that is merely a betrayal of the project. But instead, failure that is an acceptance of itself as failure — all while continuing to search, to reach, to approach the beyond.

In other words, the goal of this work includes the desire to remain unsuccessful. This is because the outcome is not supposed to be one more linguistic feature, one more theory that makes distinctions, one more fanatical totalitarian thought that would pretend once more to make the world we inhabit understandable. Any such theory would merely be a restating of the status quo, of that which already is. It would even be not just a theory, but a totalitarian feature that would by itself create and prolong reality. Any theory can do this. And it is this state of popular philosophy that is to be avoided at all cost. Especially at the cost of success.

Furthermore, any effective outcome of the question of the impossible will not be applicable, precisely because it is not to be applied. Any application would mean the mere following of a recipe, whereas for anything to be true, a break, a rupture, a beyond, it cannot be reached on the basis of an already known or even knowable process. If the beyond is to be experienced, leaving aside for a moment whether this could actually ever be the case, this would never be on the basis of any theoretical outline. Also, to even consider coming to an understanding of change that is beyond the contemporary paradigm or even beyond any paradigm at all, one thing can be clear from the beginning: there can be no content. Voicing any idea, putting any moment of happening into a structure of language, imposes the linguistic structure upon the idea. This is one of the profound problems of philosophy. For even modelling an idea into language can be killing that idea.

Still it is important for philosophy to concern itself with a conception of change, with thinking change, the beyond of that which is. At least when philosophy as an approach is used in a manner that is not merely descriptive of the present power-structure. Philosophy is meant as a method towards thinking the impossible, just as art is meant to be the method to create the impossible. While accepting the necessary failure, Derrida also confirms this, when he says, "this doesn't mean that we have to give up knowing or philosophizing: philosophical knowledge accepts this aporia as something promising and not simply negative or paralyzing."[231]

231 Jacques Derrida, *A Certain Impossible Possibility*, p.457.

This excess of jouissance that resists symbolization (logos) is the reason why in the final two decades of his teaching, Lacan (sometimes almost pathetically) insists that he considers himself an antiphilosopher, someone who rebels against philosophy: philosophy is onto-logy, its basic premise is – as Parmenides, the first philosopher, had already put it – 'thinking and being are the same': there is a mutual accord between thinking (*logos* as reason or speech) and being. Up to and including Heidegger, the Being philosophy had in mind was always the being whose house was language, the being sustained by language, the being whose horizon was opened by language; or, as Wittgenstein put it: the limits of my language are the limits of my world. Against this onto-logical premise of philosophy, Lacan focuses on the Real of jouissance as something which, though far from being simply external to language (it is rather "ex-timate" with regard to it), resists symbolization, remains a foreign kernel within it, appearing as a rupture, cut, gap, inconsistency, or impossibility.[232]

232 Slavoj Žižek, *Less Than Nothing*, p.874.

UN-ANSWERING, UN-QUESTIONING – THE VOID

"Sweet exists by convention, bitter by convention, colour by convention; atoms and Void [alone] exist in reality."
~ Democritus, *Ancilla to the Pre-Socratic Philosophers*

Thinking the impossible is the experience of the *aporia*. This is "not necessarily a failure or a simple paralysis, the sterile negativity of the impasse. It is neither stopping at it [the *aporia*, NdB] nor overcoming it. (When someone suggests to you a solution for escaping an impasse, you can almost be sure that he is ceasing to understand, assuming that he had understood anything up to that point.)"[233]

Without trying to provide solutions that would lead to yet another world that needs to be broken open, another possibility – what is left for us to do? Is it enough to develop an attitude towards thinking the impossible, without any formal structure and methodology? Would that be valuable enough? And how could we value this, but by already re-lating (re-letting) it to the world we already find ourselves in? Would our desire towards change accept such an empty solution? Empty, as it purposefully lacks any content. "The void is the supreme fullness, but man is not permitted to know it. (...) ... if they knew it in their base fashion, there would no longer be any void."[234]

Failure is an acceptance of this void. "This lack is experienced as a question insofar as every question, in order to be what it is, lacks an answer. The voice posing the question is asking the question of being, of existence, and thus of death. (...) But just as a question lacks an answer, it also demands an answer. Thus, the question opens out onto an excess of answers and thus an excess of life."[235]

233 Jacques Derrida, *Aporias*, p.32.
234 Simone Weil, *Grace and Gravity*, p.23.
235 Leonard Lawlor, *Thinking through French Philosophy*, p.124.

The void here is not an *Aufhebung* of structure. There can be no rule governing this process. "Since 'there is no rule that is applicable to chaos', chaos must first be included in the juridical order through the creation of a zone of indistinction between outside and inside, chaos and the normal situation: the state of exception."[236] According to Heidegger it is exactly through the lack, that the *real* is coming into consciousness. The thing, the Old German *dinc* referring to the coming together, the *Sammlung*, of the fourfold that makes it stay, a staying that is not a "mere persisting of something that is. Staying appropriates. It brings the four into the light of their mutual belonging. From out of staying's simple onefoldness they are betrothed, entrusted to one another. At one and thus being entrusted to one another, they are unconcealed."[237] From the void through which something becomes, it is the coming together precisely because of the void that again structures and brings it under the sphere of language, into the discourse.

The *real*, that which lies beyond language and structure, only comes into being because and through this very same structure. "As with the real in Lacan, the void or nothing that is given a place by the jug is not a natural void (nature abhors a vacuum), but an unnatural "nothingness", a "lack" that arises only *through* the structure, and only for the being who speaks: it is a lack that is produced in the symbolic order."[238] Or, to put it differently, "... the real is neither inside nor outside the symbolic, but is more like an 'internal void'."[239]

236 Giorgio Agamben, *Homo Sacer: Sovereign Power and Bare Life*, p.17.
237 Martin Heidegger, "The Thing", In: *Poetry, Language, Being*, p.171.
238 Charles Shepherdson, *Lacan and the Limits of Language*, p.8.
239 Charles Shepherdson, *Lacan and the Limits of Language*, p.8.

Accepting this internal void, the *aporia*, has not made us less despairingly feeling the essential failure of the fundamental structure of life; the paralysis of being trapped into a structure, a world, has not been alleviated. In other words, our desire is still there, lurking, longing to create a conception of the beyond, without reducing the impossible into something attainable.

Blanchot acknowledges this moving beyond the question of the impossible without posing it as a question that is answerable. He says that "if this question disappears and is forgotten, if it is taken at its word, ostensibly vanquished by discursive mastery, it is then that it prevails. Even when it presents itself in a clear form that seems to call for an answer that would conform to it, we cannot meet it except by recognizing that it poses itself as the question that is not posed."[240]

Even the voicing of the question of the impossible, is an illusion. "We believe that we think the strange and the foreign, but in reality we never think anything but the familiar; we think not the distant, but the close that measures it. And so again, when we speak of impossibility, it is possibility alone that, providing it with a reference, already sarcastically brings impossibility under its rule."[241] Any thinking of change is therefore given only to the Consumers and Followers that inhabit the worIn following Hegel, we need to distinguish the dialectical process from the circular movement of alienation and its overcoming. "This is why the verb 'failing' (…) is to be given full weight: the failure to achieve the (immediate) goal is absolutely crucial to, constitutive of, this process [of becoming] – or, as Lacan put it: *la vérité surgit de la méprise.*"[242]

240 Maurice Blanchot, *The Infinite Conversation*, p.18.
241 Maurice Blanchot, *The Infinite Conversation*, p.44.
242 Slavoj Žižek, *Less Than Nothing*, p.234.

REACHING THE IMPOSSIBLE

> "… the perfect detachment alone enables us to see things in their naked reality, outside the fog of deceptive values."
> ~ Simone Weil, *Gravity and Grace*

Accepting the failure, the *aporia* that always lies between us and the beyond, leaves us within the impossible question: What does it mean, to experience this beyond? "Even when something comes to pass as possible, when an event occurs as possible, the fact that it will have been impossible, that the possible invention will have been impossible, this impossibility continues to haunt the possibility. My relationship to the event is such that in the experience that I have of the event, the fact that it will have been impossible in its structure continues to haunt the possibility. It remains impossible; it may have taken place but it's still impossible."[243]

Bracing ourselves, not wanting to fall into the trap of tracing examples that destroy the possibility of these instances to ever become fully realised as ways to reach the beyond, let us be bold and look at what Blanchot refers to as approaching the *pas au-delà*. *Au-delà*, the beyond. That which is a step (*pas*) and which is not (*pas*) at the same time. The step into the beyond which is at the same time not beyond. And not a step. This is language at it extremity, using the ambiguity of meaning to one's advantage, saying everything at once, in one word. And not even only in French, as the Dutch language understands this ambiguity, with the same word, and takes it as its own and leads us along the ambiguity, the simultaneity of the truth-saying and perhaps even further. Perhaps, always perhaps. The Dutch *pas* is the step which is measured specifically, a stride even. But this *pas* is also the road that leads one through the mountains, on the edge of the end of the world. And this *pas* is the saying no to some-

243 Jacques Derrida, *A Certain Impossible Possibility*, p.452.

thing, to let go of one's turn, to let others go first or instead of oneself. Or to even give others the opportunity to score, to realise their dreams and goals. *Pas* is that moment that is just out of reach, that has just gone by, if you turn your head quickly you might still notice it. *Pas* is also that which is truly the case, as if you only then realise it, through the brokenness of the moment, as Heidegger could be heard saying. *Pas* is also to fit to the frame.

This is the truly *pas* beyond. The going and the not, the fitting to what is, while letting others be, go first, that moment of reaching which is – also according to time – just outside of our reach.

Let the impossible remain exactly that what it is – impossible, without refraining from approaching it. "How do we approach these passages without attempting to write the 'theory' of *le pas au-delà* through their synthesis, and then perhaps, applying the results to the guiding narrative line? How can we honor the juxtaposition of these modes of reflection with the narrative(s) while still pursuing a course of *reading* (which involves, if not method, at least some path: as indicated in the Greek *hodos*)?"[244] How can we understand and come to live with this *le pas au-delà*, which is prohibition and transgression at once, the stepping and the not-beyond in the same moment?

Two attempts will be mentioned here. They can only fail to describe, to narrate, as that is the only way to be successful – in failure. These attempts are valuable and necessary, precisely because they fail.

First of all, the experience of art and the status of poetry.

Secondly, human becoming and being human.

In a way, these two attempts cannot be distinguished, as they belong to the same domain. Yet as we need to account for the use of language, we will approach both separately, albeit that the simultaneity of the thoughts involved need to be reckoned with. Perhaps.

244 Christopher Fynsk, *Last Steps*, p.144.

THE EXPERIENCE OF ART – THE STATUS OF POETRY

"Can things take on a face? Isn't art an activity that gives things a face? Isn't the façade of a house a house that is looking at us?"
~ Emmanuel Levinas, *Isn't Ontology Fundamental?*

Let us consider art itself and the experience of art as a perhaps, a putting between brackets, possibly a manner to reach for the beyond. An experience of the impossible, while leaving it open enough to not frame the impossible as a possible.

Art itself is always present within the world, it is a part of it, while it is a part in a special manner which cannot be considered as being completely part of the world. Art is a world on its own. "Manufacturing produces an artful [*künstliche*] world of things,"[245] Hannah Arendt shared with us, while trying to expand on the human *vita activa*. This manufacturing, this bringing forth of a world of things, is what creates the world, the possible, that which is. As such art is always only a bringing forth of a world, never a world in itself.

Within all things that can be produced, brought forth, *da-gestellt*, placed in the world, art is the special category that has no goal, no use, principally nonexchangeable, and possesses no 'worth' in itself. The price one pays for it is purely arbitrarily.[246] It is what we can refer to as a work *of* art. We approach it always from our own discursive backgrounds, but the work of art itself always remains beyond our own discourse. Art has its own discourse, which is unrelated to other discourses, although it is still within the same epistemic realm.

It is as such that we can understand Heidegger's use of the word 'art' as a third entity, as a term removed from the artist and the work:

245 Hannah Arendt, *Vita Activa*, p.16.
246 See: Hannah Arendt, *Vita Activa*, p.202.

"In themselves and in their interrelations artist and work are each of them by virtue of a third thing which is prior to both, namely that which also gives artist and work of art their names—art."[247]

Defining art is not of interest to me now. Not here, not when we want to go beyond all definitions, all discursive relations, beyond the framing of the possible. We want to leave the realm of knowledge, of referring to, and of being with the discourse we find ourselves in. Whatever definition we might have of art, it will be limited to our discourse, only valid in as much as it is *mitteilbar*, as Benjamin would say. So let us not trace the history of art, or any such conceptual non-sense, as it will only give itself meaning, it will only be true within the discursive space it itself created. Therefore we will refrain from tracing the work of art through the eyes of Heidegger, Barthes, Benjamin or any of those others. However, some kind of art, some specific subset of artworks, of processes of art, could give us a clue as to how to experience the beyond.

Art is that which does not have a goal in itself. It doesn't refer to something, it has no message to tell us, and as such it lies outside the realm of language. Which doesn't mean that it cannot *also* tell us something. But precisely because it is left open, un-referential, it can break the known — it can touch both the artist who makes it, and the observer, in all kinds of ways that are not prescribed up front.

Is this beyond-experience limited to the experience of the artist herself while producing a work of art? Making, producing, creating art *could* be an experience of the beyond, a crossing of the *aporia*. This is because the work of art is not that what is produced. "The work makes public something other than itself; it manifests something other; it is an allegory. In the work of art something other is brought together with the thing that is made."[248]

247 Martin Heidegger, *Poetry, Language, Thought*, p.17.
248 Martin Heidegger, *Poetry, Language, Thought*, p.19.

Yet creating art is not a guarantee for experiencing the beyond. It is perfectly possible to create a work within the epistemic structures present, to use its material, to refer to it, for art to be a replication of the world without re-organising it. Perhaps it is safe to say a lot of so-called art doesn't reach for the beyond. It mimics, it gives an interpretation, it provides a – perhaps refreshing but nonetheless preframed – insight into matters at hand. It does not break away.

Yet there is also the experience of the observer. For her, what makes certain works of art experience the beyond? There is the experience of me as a viewer of art, the observer, the consumer of the artwork. The viewing of a work of art might be an experience of the beyond, but also this is not always the case. There are some conditions that need to be met.

Experiencing art is a personal matter, precisely because it is the viewer who does the looking, who brings her vision into it, who brings along her history and knowledge, her past experiences and her hopes for the future. We don't need to go into this much: one can turn to Hans-Georg Gadamer for a much more detailed account of this hermeneutic part of the phenomenological experience. Or to Barthes, to investigate the *punctum* that happens, sometimes. But it is important to mention, that what creates an experience of the Beyond for me, cannot be transferred to others. It is personal, while it is also universal at the same time.

But there are those works of art, that have some effect, do something. It is the work itself that brings forth something which I can then perceive. As Heidegger explains: "In the work of art the truth of an entity has set itself to work. 'To set' means here: to bring to a stand. Some particular entity, a pair of peasant shoes, comes in the work to stand in the light of its being. The being of the being comes into the steadiness of its shining."[249]

249 Martin Heidegger, *Poetry, Language, Thought*, p.35.

In the work of art, a truth-being comes into focus, where truth here needs to be understood as that which is beyond the discursive structure, beyond the material and the form of the work of art. This is not a given. It is not due to a thing being 'art', that lets this truth come about. The truth-becoming is what distinguishes between art and Art. It is not a steady characteristic of a specific work of art. Art exists in the moment of experience only.

What is interesting in this respect is the problem of reproduction, as described by Benjamin. For art to be Art and remain the work that creates a possibility of experiencing the beyond, it is important that it is presented as such. As Paul Valery remarked, describing a very modern problem when it comes to experiencing the beyond: "Just as water, gas, and electricity are brought into our houses from far off to satisfy our needs in response to a minimal effort, so we shall be supplied with visual or auditory images, which will appear and disappear at a simple movement of the hand, hardly more than a sign."[250] We need to allow for time, in order to escape it. We need to be aware when we approach it, for Art to appear and become that passageway that we are looking for.

Or, as Benjamin elaborated on the position of art within the discursive structures present in a 1916 essay entitled *On Language as Such and on the Language of Man*: "the 'essential' in a work of art involves a realm of meaning that transcends the signifying order."[251] It not only transcends the realm of language as meaning here, it breaks it open, from within.

According to many thinkers and writers, poetry is more capable — than any other form of art — of reaching the aporia. Why is this? Isn't it very dangerous to try to reach the beyond from within the world, especially when framing it through language, that framer of all frames? Are we then not always already busying ourselves with

250 Paul Valery, *Aesthetics*, p.226.
251 Christopher Fynsk, *Language & Relation*, p.177.

precisely that which we mean to let go of? Yes, of course this is true. But poetry is capable of situating the *aporia* precisely because it is just that: language. Through the experience of the limit of itself, it traverses and names what otherwise remains nameless. It is language and not devoid of meaning but also not framed and limited to language and naming as a meaning-giving. It creates a moment of lack, a gap, an *aporia*, because it is closer to the impossible than anything else. It both presents and unravels itself, it is the possible-impossible. Poetry can attain this because it is the fabric of what structures in the first place.

"The in some ways most human and wordly of the arts is poetry, whose material is language itself and whose product stays closest to the thinking that inspired it."[252] Poetry is the most human art, the art that is most closely connected to human worldliness, to the surroundings and discourses that create and make human beings. Poetry works with language itself, and stays closest to thinking, according to Hannah Arendt. But what does this mean? Is poetry somehow special precisely because it uses language?

In order to see this, let us first recall the problem of language in more detail, and what problems it gives when it comes to voicing the impossible. And then, let us afford ourselves a little detour, going into the place of poetry as art in this all, to see why time and again poetry has been given a different position when it comes to opening the epistemic structure of the world that is us.

252 Hannah Arendt, *Vita Activa*, p.205.

PROBLEM OF LANGUAGE

"Silence is the language of god, all else is poor translation."
~ Rumi

The problem of language has already been touched upon. Perhaps one could even say, it's the only thing touched upon, as this is a collection of words above anything else. Yet it is also something that cannot be said enough, as there is nothing else to say. It cannot be merely delineated and then be left alone. Language is intrinsically related to the structure we are seeking to break, and at the same time it is connected to our being human. Letting go of it would mean a disintegration of our self. When we think of the rupture of that which is, we should turn exactly to that what limits, which is language – or in the words of Wittgenstein, "The limits of my language mean the limits of my world."[253]

But is language only the referring to what we think? Language should perhaps be understood more in the manner expanded upon by Walter Benjamin, as that part of the mind that is expressible. As such it is not a framing, but an expressing. In this regard, Benjamin shows us that "[l]anguages are not strangers to one another, but are, *a priori* and apart from all historical relationships, interrelated in what they want to express."[254] This has to do with the fact that for Benjamin language is always related to life, not to human life or being *per se*, but life being everything that can have a history of its own.[255]

This question of language is confusing as there are two parts to it. Language is both referring, a signalling of what is signified, while at the same time an original relation of human being to our belonging in the world. As such, language is so much a part of our daily lives, it forms the rules and regulations that we find ourselves confronted

253 Ludwig Wittgenstein, *Tractatus Logicus-Philosophicus*, §5.6.
254 Walter Benjamin, *Illuminations*, p.72.
255 Walter Benjamin, *Illuminations*, p.70-72.

with, that are set in place, and are very clearly discernible in the educational aspect in which human beings are being made to adhere to the specific rules. This is what Nietzsche referred to as *language as translation of our experience into the familiar*. "The whole notion of an 'inner experience' enters our consciousness only after it has found a language that the individual understands – i.e., a translation of a situation into a familiar situation – 'to understand,' naïvely put merely means: to be able to express something old and familiar."[256]

But language is also the place where the multiplicity of being is maintained. It is in this sense that Jacques Derrida says: "for any translation into [another] language would lose something of its potential multiplicity."[257]

When we want to talk about the event, that experience of radical rupture of the possible, when we want to say the event, we are also confronted by this dual nature of language. Language is on the one hand constitutive of what is, shaping, creating. And, on the other hand, language is performative; it is a showing forth, a representing, a bringing into relation, a bringing forth of what is expressible in the world. Language is thus a creating.

Saying the event, that moment of breaking, is a symptom of this problematic relationship between the constitutive and performative aspects of language. "I propose the word symptom as another term, beyond the telling of the truth or the performativity that produces the event. The event defeats both the constative and the performative, the 'I know' and the 'I think'."[258]

It is this paradox that language itself embodies: that when the impossible is named, it loses its power of being truly *other*. So, the impossible is always a pre-linguistic notion, something that is prior

256 Friedrich Nietzsche, *Werke in drei Bänden*, 3, p.805, as quoted by Paul de Man, *Allegories of Reading*, p.108.
257 Jacques Derrida, *Aporias*, p.9.
258 Jacques Derrida, *A Certain Impossible Possibility*, p. 456.

to coming into being. As Blanchot explains: "But must we not also say: impossibility, neither negation nor affirmation, indicates what in being has always already *preceded* being and yields to no ontology? Certainly, we must! Which amounts to the presentiment that it is again being that awaits in possibility, and that if it negates itself in possibility, it is in order better to preserve itself from this *other* experience that always precedes it and is always more initial than the affirmation that names being. This would be the experience that the Ancients no doubt revered under the title of Destiny: that which diverts from every destination and that we are seeking to name more directly in speaking of the *neutral*."[259]

Why is this so? Derrida gives a few reasons that show why saying the event cannot be considered constitutive. First, the cognitive saying of the event is always done afterwards, after the event, the break, the rupture, has already taken place. Secondly, the language in which it is said is repetitive, a measure of generality: therefore, never part of the singularity of the event. Finally, it is important to notice the political factor: the saying of the event is never reliable, there is always already interpretation, it is a conclusion based on a framing of a selection of what is being said and what is left out. "The political vigilance that this calls for on our part obviously consists in organizing a critical examination of all the mechanisms that hold out the appearance of saying the event when they are in fact making it, interpreting and producing it."[260]

If saying the event can never be constitutive of it, can language be performing the event? Derrida focuses on specific events here that are directly related to a linguistic event, that form a rupture of the present, like confession, promise, oath, and giving – in the sense of a giving thanks that annuls the gift. "

259 Maurice Blanchot, *The Infinite Conversation*, p.47.
260 Jacques Derrida, *A Certain Impossible Possibility*, p.47.

This means – to go quickly – that the gift as a gift is possible only when it appears impossible."[261] Just as you can only forgive the impossible.

> Forgiving, if it is possible, can only come to be as impossible. But this impossibility is not simply negative. This means that the impossible must be done. The event, if there is one, consists in doing the impossible. But when someone does the impossible, if someone does the impossible, no one, above all not the doer of the deed, is in a position to adjust a self-assured, theoretical statement to the event and say, 'this happened' or 'forgiveness has taken place' or 'I've forgiven'.[262]

That is why the saying of the event is precisely not that; not the breaking, not even in a performative manner. "A statement such as 'I forgive' or 'I've forgiven' is absurd, and, moreover, it's obscene."[263] And, as such, acknowledging the event, stating that this or that was an event, or that one has taken part of an event is a betrayal of the intended impossibility. "How can I be sure that I have the right to forgive and that I've effectively forgiven rather than forgotten, or overlooked, or reduced the offense to something forgivable? I can no more say, 'I forgive' than 'I give'. These are impossible statements. I can always make them, but in doing so, I betray what I mean to say. I'm not saying anything. I should never be able to say, 'I'm giving' or 'I'm forgiving'."[264]

This is exactly what Blanchot refers to when he says that language kills, by naming.[265] We could say, that by naming, we don't confront exactly that which appears to us as impossible. Instead, by naming, we signify the possibility of destruction. "My language does not kill anyone. But, [in saying 'this woman'] if this woman were not

261 Jacques Derrida, *A Certain Impossible Possibility*, p.49.
262 Jacques Derrida, *A Certain Impossible Possibility*, p.449-50.
263 Jacques Derrida, *A Certain Impossible Possibility*, p.450.
264 Jacques Derrida, *A Certain Impossible Possibility*, p.450
265 Maurice Blanchot, *Works of Fire*, p.323.

really capable of dying, is she were not threatened by death at every moment of her life, bound and united to it by an essential bond, I would not be able to accomplish that ideal negation, that deferred assassination that is my language."[266]

But is there then only one thing to conclude from this all? Is our linguistic being, our always already being entangled in language as the House of Being, preventing us from saying anything about the event, and from saying the event? Or can we move beyond this, can we reach for the event, the breaking, even through and precisely because of language?

"Every time that saying the event exceeds this dimension of information, knowledge, and cognition, it enters the night (…) the 'night of non-knowing', something that's not merely ignorance, but that no longer pertains to the realm of knowledge. A non-knowing that is not lack, not sheer obscurantism, ignorance, or non-science, but simply something that is not of the same nature as knowing. A saying the event that produces the event beyond the confines of knowledge. This kind of saying is found in many experiences where, ultimately, the possibility that such and such an event will happen appears impossible."[267]

This infinite, abyssal movement where language reaches a limit is not a point where everything stops. "Rather, it is a site of engagement and passage where reflection halts, but in becoming the approach to/of the outside. It is a threshold, in this sense, but a threshold already marked by a crossing, a passage, that Derrida has identified and engaged in exemplary fashion by tracking the *pas* (both adverb of negation and noun: 'step') that echoes throughout Blanchot's texts."[268]

266 Maurice Blanchot, *Works of Fire*, p.313.
267 Jacques Derrida, *A Certain Impossible Possibility*, p.448.
268 Christopher Fynsk, *Language & Relation*, p.240.

This is what the oath does, what forgiving does. The language of a binding oneself to the other, the ultimate promise. It is performative, it creates what it names.[269] But the moment we want to describe, to understand the oath, the impossibility of it is degraded to a mundane level of everydayness. The moment language describes and reaches for understanding, the impossibility of the performative function disappears.

Language thus limits and prevents us from saying the event, when language is the referring to what-is, as a way towards knowing. Yet there is a performative aspect that might be able to break this language-meaning-referring-structure, that makes language a witness of the event, albeit not constitutive. Which is why it is important to acknowledge the existence of *poetry*, which is an act of saying the event without becoming part of the discourse of knowing. Poetry as the saying of precisely that which is impossible to say. Poetry as an experience outside and within language.

269 Giorgio Agamben, *The Sacrament of Language*, p.55.

POSSIBILITY OF LANGUAGE

> "To will the interruption of the discourse (...) is not only to 'affirm the break'; it is to will something that communicates or affirms itself in that break."
> ~ Christopher Fynsk, *Language & Relation*

There is thus an important role for poetic language when it comes to the overcoming of the dichotomy of impossibility-possibility. It does not create a third category, but it leaves the realm of this dichotomy nonetheless. "Poetry is not there in order to say impossibility: it simply answers to it, saying in responding. Such is the secret lot, the secret decision of every essential speech in us: naming the possible, responding to the impossible."[270] It is a responding to the impossible as the other – an important movement, to which we will have to come back later.

By naming the impossible it becomes possible: it is killed, and it frames the frame in order to un-frame. However, this naming in poetry is not the same as a naming as referring, or a naming as defining. In poetry the names are used despite the fact that they are names. It is only when the naming-as-referring mechanism is let go of — which is what is meant when we refer to 'poetic' language — that this breaking, this responding to the call of the impossible, takes place. It is no wonder that Heidegger talks about truly human life as poetic, as it refers precisely to this instance of responding to the call for truth-beyond-world, that is established the throbbing pulse of what is human, and which is the event that takes place in a work of art.

Levinas also refers to this breaking, this pointing of the poetic to the unsayable: "the poets and philosophers force, for a moment, its inexpressible essence."[271] This poetic breaking is at once both personal

270 Maurice Blanchot, *The Infinite Conversation*, p.48.
271 Emmanuel Levinas, *The Trace of the Other*, p.346.

and human. Remember that language needs to be seen as the plural sphere, which according to Blanchot requires a writing for the coming into being of its thought. "In the plural sense of a language that breaks from the gathering *logos* and the grasp of the concept, categories such as singular, general, or universal must obviously be rethought."[272] Within writing, or poetry more specifically, the names that are used that do not refer to what is already always there make it impossible to take poetry as sheer fact, as a scientific text that is limited and clear in the way it refers-to-the-world. Poetic writing instead is to be seen as holding "the possibility of a radical transformation, be it for *one alone*, that is to say, his suppression as a personal existence."[273]

So, what does it mean to respond to the impossible?

Naming the possible, responding to the impossible. Responding does not consist in formulating an answer, in such a way as to appease the question that would obscurely come from such a region; even less in transmitting, in the manner of an oracle, a few truth contents of which the daytime world would not yet have knowledge. It is poetry's existence, each time it is poetry, that in itself forms a response and, in this response, attends to what is addressed to us in impossibility (by turning itself away). Poetry does not express this, does not say it, does not draw it under the attraction of language. But it responds. Every beginning speech begins by responding; a response to what is not yet heard, an attentive response in which the impatient waiting for the unknown and the desiring hope for presence are affirmed.[274]

So, while poetry is not saying the impossible, it is responding to it, by moving away from the overpowering realm of language, moving away from delineating an answer – just like the question is unable to

272 Christopher Fynsk, *Last Steps*, p.129.
273 Maurice Blanchot, *The Step Not Beyond*, p.1-2.
274 Maurice Blanchot, *The Infinite Conversation*, p.48.

phrase the longing for the impossible without limiting the possible answer, the response is similarly a mere pointing without framing. It is this response that is also the human becoming of the one that experiencing this longing for the beyond.

According to Heidegger, poets should be seen as people who take language and bend it to their own needs, not being limited by the structures given by society, by *das Man.* Poets and philosophers are the guardians of that space in which poetic language locates itself, the space which creates the possibility of response, of human being. "Language is the house of being [*Die Sprache ist das Haus des Seins*]. In its home human beings dwell. Those who think and those who create with words are the guardians of this home. Their guardianship accomplishes the manifestation of being insofar as they bring this manifestation to language and preserve it in language through their saying."[275] What is important here is the distinction between language as discursive realm, and speech as the instance of language in which it is experienced and a response. Speech is always that moment of responding to something, external or internal. It is this speech that *can* be located outside of the world, outside of *das Man*. This performative character of speech is what is capable of the breaking, of the sense-less, of madness.

Yet when thinking becomes a technique, language itself becomes an instrument; part and constitutive of the discursive realm, the discourse. When language is faced with providing efficient communication in the public realm, language is lost in *das Man,* the 'they'. Heidegger writes about this type of language, when it is lost to the epistemic power of the possible: "Language thereby falls into the service of expediting communication… language comes under the dictatorship of the public realm, which decides in advance what is intelligible and what must be rejected as unintelligible."[276]

275 Martin Heidegger, *Letter on Humanism*, p.239.
276 Martin Heidegger, *Letter on Humanism*, p.242.

When language stops referring, stops being a carrier of signification, it opens up for the possibility of the beyond. "The sign is made from afar, from beyond and in the beyond. Poetic language gives sign without the sign being a bearer of signification through relinquishing signification."[277] Which is why Blanchot writes "Literature says: 'I no longer represent, I am; I do not signify, I present.'"[278]

Therefore, we once and for all have to let go of Wittgenstein's mysticism, "his believing that one can *show* when one cannot *speak*. But without language, nothing can be shown. And to be silent is still to speak. Silence is impossible. That is why we desire it. Writing (or Telling, as distinct from anything written or told) precedes every phenomenon, every manifestation or show: all appearing."[279]

Thus, what is required is not just poetry, it is a specific type of poetry. It is perhaps what comes close to what Blanchot has labelled 'mad writing'. Writing in this sense cannot be seen as a merely reflecting of what is, as a putting into effect of the discursive structures. As Blanchot says, "writing alone (…), on the condition that discourse, having accomplished itself as logos, withdraw from it every seat from which it might declare itself or sustain itself, and expose him to the menace, the vain prestige of what no one would henceforth dare to name: mad writing."[280]

Or, as Fynsk extols: "The task has barely opened in its exigency: to write *without* the grounding present, to affirm relation to the future *save* for the present that holds all promise of 'peace' hostage to its self-reference."[281] In other words, whenever we write within the present, we affirm what is, even the words that are used to try and break away from it are only referring back to the discourse within which we find ourselves. We need to have an open relationship, in

277 Emmanuel Levinas, *Sur Maurice Blanchot*, p. 39.
278 Maurice Blanchot, *The Gaze of Orpheus*, p. 47
279 Maurice Blanchot, *The Writing of Disaster*, p.11.
280 Maurice Blanchot, *The Step Not Beyond*, p.22.
281 Christopher Fynsk, *Last Steps*, p.187.

writing, through writing, despite the limits that are made visible in writing, as language.

This mad writing, the poetic, concerns itself with writing words despite the very nature of words. Precisely because of the use of the foundation of what is framing us, it can show this break. In this way mad writing is, and will always be more than any other type of art can ever accomplish. Music can stir the soul, and the momentary experience of a piece of music in the right circumstances, can move a person deeply. But it does not break. It lets you experience something that may inspire, that may move you to change your life. But it does not break away from the very thing that it represents. It does not point towards something that lies both inside and beyond the very sequences of tones, beyond the image (re)produced. It touches upon what one already is, what one already knows. It will remind of a past experience, it will let you recognise something that one experienced before. It will call to mind something other than that which is presented, yet it is not a beyond, it goes not beyond the hermeneutical relationship of the subject with the object.

Mad writing does break. It leaves one utterly left alone, it destroys precisely because it does not refer to the signs that it is made of, and which refer to what once was. It is that very thing that it is, that it has always been, that is responsible for the frame. And therefore, the break can be full, can be radical. We should not appropriate the poem first, to analyse it as the literary scientists prefer to do. Approaching the poem as a referring to something else makes the poem into just one more form of representation of the world. Approaching the impossible that is the poem concerns itself with taking the poem as it is; approaching it by itself, without context, without a full extensive knowledge that only distracts, that would only make you analyse what is presented.

BECOMING HUMAN

> "Thus the sense that community, in its very failure, is linked to a certain kind of writing, a writing that has nothing else to seek than the last words: Come, come for you whom injunction, prayer, waiting are unfitting."
> ~ Maurice Blanchot, *The Unavowable Community*

The impossible is not dependent on language. It is precisely the un-relatedness to the world that makes the impossible valuable. Therefore, we need to reconsider how everything relates, our desire, our framing, our limiting. Let us start from the beginning. As always, we find ourselves stuck in formulating an answer to a question that is frames through the frame itself. We need to move back, step back, trace back, let go of the figures of speech, of the thoughts that have filled the bubble that needed to be empty to burst it in the first place.

As we long for the impossible, the subsequent despair keeps us from attaining it. We long for a change, a breaking free from the world that is radical enough not to be noticed. We are submerged in metaphysical murmurings here. 'Change' as a breaking, a rupture, refers to a becoming of something that was not. It leads us back to the question of what it means to be, the ultimate question that always must be thought again. Names, egos, authority, thoughts, let them not distract us for one minute.

We are right back at the centre of things, that centre that is only there because it is us, our selves that are placed there. It is the human, it is that which goes beyond all that is constrained by the world. Impossible, change, rupture. The reaching for it is all about what it means to *become*. What it means to *think*, to *be*.

Thinking is the path of becoming. It is to be associated with the mouth. Truly thinking is to be eating, digesting. Philosophy is the embellishment, the focusing on the most fundamental digestive system. That what one eats is what one becomes. The true philosopher is not someone who repeats what she has eaten. She is what she has become. For her it is impossible to distinguish between her own thoughts and the thoughts of others, as they are all part of reality, equally important for the process of becoming. How can one distinguish between what one is, and one's food that has led to this being? Food is transformed, but only in as far as it was food it will be accepted. The rest is made into faeces and extracted from the body. That what was once food, is now indistinguishably linked to what is. Human.

And as we eat, we become. We chew, we break mouthfuls of structure. We incorporate that what resonates even though it is not us. We become only that what we control. Eating something that is too similar to what we are is looked at with distrust, disgust. But reaching for the impossible means going even beyond cannibalism. All the resistance that is wired into the societal structures that keep us occupied with the present state of being, all the voices that keep us from reaching for the impossible, all the self-help-books that keep us from failing, need to be disregarded. Gutted out of our system. To be un-seen, not-seen. To be disowned, to stop it being a part of the *status quo*.

We need to breathe freely, to move beyond the life as we know it. It is time to inspire, to breathe-in, related to spirit, *espirit spiritus spirare pneuma*, that ghost of truth that haunts and that inhibits and inhabits human beings.

Let us repeat this not merely in order to repeat this. Because repeating what others have said, tracing their words, their faeces, is not enough to actually become. One can only become by oneself, to become. Remembering, relating to the past or the future is not original becoming. Only the present gives enough space, enough openness for humans to become.

This eternal repeating of the same, this "*Éternel Retour du Même*"[282], is what is closely related to becoming. It is *not* being a Follower and following the trace, it is *not* being trapped in the illusion of progression, of progress, of a better place that is just around the corner. It is a repeating to return. To return to what is original, which has always already been, but never became.[283] The impossible, the original cannot be actualised. It is always laying beyond, feeding our despair, our desire. Becoming human is not to succeed in the ways of the world, is not to invent what was already invented. It is to see that which is other. That what is truly me.

282 Maurice Blanchot, *Le pas au-delà*, p.21.
283 See: Gilles Deleuze, *Difference & Repetition*.

BECOMING IS NOT ACTUALISING THE IMPOSSIBLE

> "In all fiction, when a man is faced with alternatives, he chooses one at the expense of others. In the almost unfathomable Ts'ui Pên, he chooses — simultaneously — all of them... In Ts'ui Pên's work, all the possible solutions occur, each one being the point of departure for other bifurcations."
> ~ Jorge Luis Borges, *A Personal Anthology*

Some things need to be said over and over, in order to be given the space it deserves, and before it can be done blindly. How can we reach for the impossible without making the impossible attainable? To do so, let us trace the argument of Quentin Meillassoux, which is a bold attempt to face one of the most fundamental questions in philosophy, namely the problem of induction, the problem of grounding causal connection. This is what the question of the impossible comes down to, the fact that something that exists always needs to be linked to what precedes it, that it has this causal connection. The question and the necessity of breaking this connection, is what the quest for the impossible is about. Let us open up this question, to see where Meillassoux takes us, in order to come back to wherever it was we started.

Meillassoux approaches the question from the assumption that there is a Multiple, which cannot be reduced to a One. He introduces the notion of virtuality, following in the footsteps of Deleuze. "Virtuality (...) designates a situation in which one cannot totalize the set of possibles, so that something new emerges, a case is realized for which there was no place in the pre-existing set of possibles."[284] Note here, that this assumes already that the set of possibles cannot be totalized, the totality of the possible cannot be pointed out. This

284 Slavoj Žižek, *Less Than Nothing*, p.229.

is however problematic, as the total set of possibles is not limited to our understanding or ability to realise it. The episteme within we find ourselves, is precisely that: a totalised set of possibles. Although Žižek is right to argue that this does not mean that when we posit some New which "cannot be fully accounted for by the set of its pre-existing conditions, this does not mean that we have encountered a limitation of our knowledge, our inability to understand the 'higher' reason is at work here."[285] He is right. The limit of our knowledge would mean the limit of our discourse, whereas the episteme also accounts for that which lies beyond the pre-existent conditions. It is however wrong to conclude from this, as Meillassoux does, that this leads to "accede to the ineffectivity of an All of potentialities which would pre-exist their [the novelties'] emergence."[286] The fact that first reality is assumed in the form of a multitude – which is nothing other than realising that although we experience a One, this is merely a discourse within the Multitude worlds in the epistemic reality – and limited according to a specific ontology, makes this conclusion impossible to take seriously. It might be that there is not this 'All' that is knowable, nor that we even need it to know or posit for our ontology to function. Yet this does not 'prove' anything. We cannot logically deduce the non-existence of an All, merely because we have to deal with the virtualMeillassoux's argument therefore does not hold, except for within human experience, within the structures of reality in which we find ourselves already. "Time creates the possible at the very moment it makes it come to pass, it brings forth the possible as it does the real, it inserts itself in the very throw of the die, to bring forth a seventh case, in principle unforeseeable, which breaks the fixity of potentialities."[287]

285 Slavoj Žižek, *Less Than Nothing*, p.231.
286 Quentin Meillassoux, *Potentiality and Virtuality*, p.80.
287 Quentin Meillassoux, *Potentiality and Virtuality*, p.74.

For materialists, as for idealists, the real and the possible are one. The virtual is then just a way to account for the moment in which something that we were not yet aware of, something that was not accounted for within the set of possibles, comes into being, becomes actual. Realists need to explain the coming into existence of this 'new', but only because they posit that the All, everything, is equal to the virtual, the knowable. This cognivist approach to the episteme is problematic.

Meillassoux concludes that "every radical rupture of the present in relation to the past becomes the manifestation of the absence of any order capable of overseeing the chaotic power of becoming."[288] The problem here is that the assumption that reality consists of a multiple which cannot be totalised, is here merely confirmed. Yet this cannot be taken as a proof, that this totalisation, such as for instance an idea of 'God' in the conservative sense, needs be disregarded. The 'miracle' that emerges, the actualisation of that for which there is no pre-existing possibility, should not be taken as a manifestation of the inexistence of a totality, but merely an actualisation of a previously mere potential.

In other words, the actualisation of the impossible into a possible, does not make the impossible itself disappear. Nor does it mean that the impossible has become possible. Nor does it mean that any new is an actualisation of an impossible – for what lies outside of one's discourse can still be unknowingly part of the present episteme. The impossible as impossible remains precisely that, the beyond. It does not strictly appear, although it can seem so, precisely because of the virtual reality that lies beyond that which is already within the present.

288 Quentin Meillassoux, *Potentiality and Virtuality*, p.75.

A problem with Meillassoux's approach to account for the emergence of a New, is the direct relation the New continues to have with the realm of the possible. This is always going to be the case, so it does not make sense to deny this as Meillassoux seems to do. He pretends to delineate some ability to create a radical New that is un-related to the previous state. Rolling a die and getting a seven, is still relying on the roll of the die in the first place. Meillassoux confirms that "time throws the die, but only to shatter it, to multiply its faces, beyond any calculus of possibilities."[289] Yet he does not account for thinking in a structure that is beyond the structure within possibilities are already thought. Seven is still a real number. He merely confirms the structures that are already in place. A saying 'no' to a specific limitation – such as saying there are not merely six sides of a die – does not shatter the framework, the epistemic framework, within which the die has presented itself to us in the first place.

Nietzsche poses the same kind of critique. "Nietzsche reproaches modern atheism precisely for the fact that, in it, the 'big Other' survives – true, no longer as the substantial God, but as the totalizing symbolic frame of reference."[290] Nietzsche is right: the episteme and the consequential totalizing frame that it imposes upon everyone still needs to be understood as (a) 'God', as the substance that "guarantees the meaningful consistency of the universe."[291] What we need is the interfact.[292] However, following the call that Nietzsche continues to make, it is precisely the work in which the humanness of the human being is established, in continuing to let go of this totalising frame. This is the dangerous *perhaps* that Nietzsche establishes and which he calls upon us to embrace.

289 Quentin Meillassoux, *Potentiality and Virtuality*, p.74.
290 Slavoj Žižek, *Less Than Nothing*, p.232.
291 Slavoj Žižek, *Less Than Nothing*, p.232.
292 See: Gabriel Yoran, *The Interfact.*

The human being that has actively killed this God and the framework that it carries inside itself, that actively searches and reaches for the beyond, that is the human being because of whom and for whom we can say that the totalitarian God has truly died.

Meillassoux's problem then seems to be the disregarding of the essentially *human* of the *becoming* of the new. He has not killed the One. God lives on in his structures. The virtual does not solve anything beyond showing the limits of discourse. It does not lead us to the impossible that requires failure.

Actualising, totalising. Let us not be distracted, distraught. Letting go of the epistemic frame, accepting the failure, approaching the beyond without actualising it, is the moment of becoming, of being human.

BEING HUMAN AS EXPERIENCING THE IMPOSSIBLE

"...the human being is the inhuman; the one whose humanity is completely destroyed is the one who is truly human."
~ Giorgio Agamben, Remnants of Auschwitz

Not actualising, we stay in the present. The moment is there, the only moment one can speak of. Reaching for the impossible, that moment of rupture that may or may not lead to actual change, the break that is independent of its consequences, that cannot be judged or seen. *Sauf*, as Blanchot[293] would say: 'except' – *ausser*, *behalve* – *sauf* through and within experience. It is this placing outside, that also locates, that also mistakenly puts the impossible in words, and thus removes itself from this moment.

Yet the striving, even while facing the necessary failure, or precisely because of this failure, is what makes the human. Why does the impossible do this? What makes it a human undertaking, what is meant with human, and what does it mean, to always want to define this human-ness? Is it just another framing, another manner in which to destroy the possibility of the outside? We will need to face this violence, this utter-ness that leaves us devoid of the capacity to relate. This is the utter, these are the udders that leaves you other, the always already being-woman.[294]

Reaching the beyond as the project of becoming human is in and by itself not an original project. It has been done before and it will need to be done continuously. It is what Nietzsche had in mind, when he wrote about the becoming of the *super*-man.

293 Maurice Blanchot, *Le pas au-delà*, p.16.
294 Personal conversation with Antonia Grousdanidou, 2014.

Nietzsche writes about how philosophy in this new time has become the saying-no to the world: "one's own saying-no-to-the-world, enemy to life, destructing of the senses, un-sensing aloofness attitude of the philosophers",[295] has for the longest time not been possible ("*gar nicht möglich*") except when thinking oneself outside of what one is, as a self-misunderstanding, "*ein Selbst-Missverständniss*".[296] His question is therefore an important one: is being human, a 'philosopher', now truly possible in this world; is there enough courage and will, self-knowledge, enough "*Stolz, Wagniss, Tapferkeit, Selbstgewissheit, Wille des Geistes, Wille zur Verantwortlichkeit, Freiheit des Willens vorhanden*"?[297] Interestingly, these attitudes that Nietzsche encourages and defines as the basis of a thinking, are not limited to the what-is: Pride, daring, courage, self-confidence, will of the spirit, will for responsibility, and most of all, freedom of will.

What is important to note is that Nietzsche talks about the philosopher as someone who already is, who has already attained the status of reaching the beyond, of the saying no to what is. Zarathustra already reached the place outside the market square. He talks to us from up on the mountain. Which is not to say we just need to locate that mountain and we will be fine. No: the beyond when visualised and knowable like this, is only an illusion. The mountain is merely a symbol of the beyond. A taking literally, a framing of the impossible, would limit our ability to reach it. Many have walked into the trap and become followers of this ideal, this metaphor, and thereby destroyed the impossibility it may hold. But as Nietzsche has foreseen this, he tells us in strong language: go ahead and away from me, protect yourself from my Zarathustra. He is aware that he is only one more illusion that will lead, has led, will continue to lead us astray.[298]

295 Friedrich Nietzsche, *Jenseits von Gut und Böse*, p.378.
296 Friedrich Nietzsche, *Jenseits von Gut und Böse*, p.378.
297 Friedrich Nietzsche, *Jenseits von Gut und Böse* , p.361.
298 See: Friedrich Nietzsche, *Ecce Homo*, p.4.

Again and again Nietzsche warns us against the dangerous old play of notions ("*gefährliche alte Begriffs-Fabelei*") such as '*reine Vernunft*' and '*Erkenntnisse an sich*', that require us to think that which cannot be thought. We should keep our eyes occupied with seeing-something, instead of seeing with the eyes of an illusionary objectivity, with the eyes of a so-called Big Other that has the power to incorporate interpretative powers. As Nietzsche exclaims:

> The *only* seeing we have is seeing from a perspective; the *only* knowledge we have is knowledge from a perspective; and *the more* emotions we allow to be expressed in words concerning something, *the more* eyes, different eyes, we know how to train on the same thing, the more complete our 'idea' of this thing, our 'objectivity' will be. But to eliminate the will in general, to suspend all our emotions without exception—even if we were capable of that—what would that be? Wouldn't we call that castrating the intellect?[299]

What does this mean, for our longing of the beyond? Does it not say, that the more we see with the eyes of others or with any eyes that are pre-framed, even our own eyes, the more we approach reality through the understanding of concepts that are posited within the world as it is, approaching it through and from within the epistemic space, the further away we are from being a philosopher? When we take upon ourselves the reality of this world as it is, we have castrated our intellect, as Nietzsche says. I would take it even further, as it is not our intellect that is what makes the beyond available. Is it not the case that all the understandings and notions of this world are contained within our intellect? When we limit our human-being to our being-intellect, are we not limiting the beyond from the beginning, are we not framing ourselves to be our own obstacle when it comes to arriving at the beyond? Therefore, the reaching, the longing for the beyond is exactly non-intellectual.

---

299 Friedrich Nietzsche, *Jenseits von Gut und Böse*, p.365.

The seeing with our own eyes instead of with the eyes of others, makes our longing not only truly personal, it makes the looking for the beyond a radically personal and solitary experience. Arriving at this state of independence is not only the beginning of philosophy, but it is the beginning of being human. It is the acceptance of belonging to the world we are thrown into, while at the same time acknowledging that this belonging is also what keeps us from being, from being and becoming human. The moment the child develops an understanding of the 'I', it becomes conscious and for the first time will experience what it means to be human, to be alone. "All that is form, system, category, frame or plan tends to make things absolute and springs from a lack of inner energy, from a sterile spiritual life."[300] In other words, there is something more outside of the framing-intellect. There is the human being that is breaking free from this framing. It is, as Nietzsche confirms, the attaining of the highest goal: the reaching of and for the impossible, the ultimate deliverance itself, the becoming free from 'knowing', 'truth' and 'being' as "an emancipation from all delusions, as 'knowledge', as 'truth', as 'being', as the removal of all goals, all wishes, all acts, and thus as a place beyond good and evil. Good and evil, are both fetters: the perfect one became master over both."[301]

What we should, however, be aware of is that this experience of the impossible is not a state one can attain and then be done with. It is not that once we reach the beyond – whatever that may mean, the state of the '*Vollendete*' as Nietzsche calls it, the nirvana, the sainthood, the real, the truly human; but let us not put it into words other than calling it the 'beyond', in order not to limit it – we can think we are done, that we can be proud of ourselves, of what we have attained. This type of pride rejoices in belonging to the world, in consuming and following, and this is not the type of pride Nietzsche referred to, when he called for pride and courage. Instead, we are looking and

300 Emil Cioran, *On the Heights of Despair*, p.59.
301 Friedrich Nietzsche, *Jenseits von Gut und Böse*, p.380.

searching for a state that enables a proudness of knowing that one is always only approaching the beyond, facing the impossible, as an ever-continuing struggle with that what one already knows. Once a method of deliverance is described and therefore prescribed by those who have used it successfully, it has already stopped being true.[302] Which is why Nietzsche encourages us to find our own Zarathustra in *Ecce Homo*, one of his last works left to us – which was meant to be only the beginning of a re-evaluations of all values, a re-thinking of truth, a re-working of reality. It is as Derrida reminds us: "When someone suggests to you a solution for escaping an impasse, you can almost be sure that he is ceasing to understand, assuming that he had understood anything up to that point."[303]

How are we to understand that this searching for the beyond is what makes us human? Nietzsche alludes to this, in the last paragraph from his *Zur Genealogie der Moral*, when he shows that when man does not take the ideal of searching for this beyond seriously, the animal we call man has no goal, no meaning [*keinen Sinn*]. There is no meaning for animal-human life, it is "*Umsonst!*" Or, as Cioran puts it: "I am: therefore the world is meaningless."[304] But this failure of there being something concrete, this void in the animal-human condition, which one cannot explain or put into words, is what is the origin of this failure, these pains of being. It is not the running away from this suffering that makes the animal-human into human. The suffering regarding the being-without-sense, not the senseless suffering, is what leaves us with the nihilism that kills all that is human.[305] With this suffering, *will* itself was saved. "...man will sooner will *nothingness,* than *not* will."[306]

302 See also: Hemann Hesse, *Siddhartha.*
303 Jacques Derrida, *Aporias*, p.32.
304 Emil Cioran, *On the Heights of Despair*, p.31.
305 Friedrich Nietzsche, *Zur Genealogie der Moral*, p.429.
306 Friedrich Nietzsche, *Jenseits von Gut und Böse*, p.412.

The impossible is therefore related directly to *being* human as opposed to being animal-human, the being thrown into *das Mann*, the everydayness of the world, being prisoned in the epistemological space. The impossible, precisely because it lies outside of this space, outside of the knowable, makes the impossible not inhabited by the animal-human, the body, the worldliness – but leaves it open for and to the indestructibility of the being-human. As Blanchot tells us: "Should we then say: impossibility is being itself? Certainly, we must! Which amounts to recognizing in possibility the sovereign power to negate being: man, each time that he is on the basis of possibility, is the being without being. The struggle for possibility is this struggle against being."[307] We are only human insofar we are (be) longing to the impossible.

It is thus that we have to reach for the impossible as a tentative approach to *become* human. It is the leaving behind of the epistemic space, that which we have defined as human but which is only animal-human, intellectual and scientific. Becoming human is an essential element of this reaching of the beyond. "Becoming isn't part of history; history amounts only to the set of preconditions, however recent, that one leaves behind in order to "become," that is, to create something new."[308] There is, therefore, no human history. There is only a history of the world, of the epistemic structures, or perspectives of reality. The human is always outside of time, of framing.

Becoming can as such be seen as relating to the Lacanian Real. According to Judith Butler, the Real for Lacan is twofold: both presymbolic (thus before the linguistic, outside of the epistemic space) and post-symbolic, as emerging as a void within the symbolic, the episteme. "The category of the real is needed", because we must provide a more adequate account of what remains 'outside' discourse, what is 'foreclosed' from the symbolic order – since "what is refused

307 Maurice Blanchot, *The Infinite Conversation*, p.47.
308 Gilles Deleuze, *Negotiations*, p. 170-171.

or repudiated in the formation of the subject continues to determine that subject.""[309] Becoming is thus an essential relationship of the subject who is not yet subject, to the pre-linguistic structure, that which is outside of discourse, foreclosed from the symbolic order: the impossible.

Yet we need to take a turn from the singleness that forms part of the Nietzschean movement. After the Shoah, the ethical realm cannot be set apart from any notion of what it means to be or to become human. There is always already a relationship to the other that I need to account for, by being human. Either by accepting the difference, or by accepting the repetition of the essential movement of becoming.

The longing for the impossible, the desire that moves one to *become human*, is a call for response, an essential trait of human life that is response-ability, the ability to respond to this call. This call for becoming human, of our response-ability to this call, for the arrival of the impossible, is something shared among human beings: "This im-possible is not privative. It is not the inaccessible, and it is not what I can indefinitely defer: it is announced to me, sweeps down upon me, precedes me, and seizes me *here now*, in a nonvirtualizable way, in actuality and not potentiality... This im-possible is thus not a regulative *idea* or *ideal*. It is what is most undeniably real. Like the other. Like the irreducible and nonappropriable difference of the other."[310] It is precisely this *other* that is at the same time the abyss and the ground upon which the impossible is based.

---

309 Judith Butler, *Bodies that Matter*, p.189-190.
310 Jacques Derrida, *Deconstructing Terrorism*, p.134

THE OTHER, AUTRUI

> "How, then, can one pretend to acquit oneself of the 'event' in speaking of luck or chance, a word immediately reduced to its indigency, especially when the other is *at stake* there?"
> ~ Maurice Blanchot, *The Step Not Beyond*

Being human, becoming human, precisely the approaching of the impossible, is both grounded in the present and in the overcoming of it. It is radical alterity presenting itself. It is in facing the *other*, the *autrui*, that the present is shown in the most intense manner, in a manner in which the reaching beyond is central. "The visitation of [the other, the *autrui*] is then not the disclosure of a world."[311] It is precisely *not* the disclosure, as it is the rupturing, the breaking of the same that never transcends. It is this breaking despite its paradoxical trapping in the present, in the world, in being ever regarded as the same precisely as it is becoming, as it is always already the same and the new.

What then is this *other*? And how are we to understand this relation between the I and the *other*? When we encounter a phenomenon, this encounter makes us already interrelated. The world is always already there, and with it also the *other*, that which is devoid of any structuring worldliness, that is always already there, waiting for us to be seen, to be face-d. This Levinassian idea of the 'other', is focusing on how the 'face' of the other is always already asking something of us, the observer. 'Face' here is not the body, not the muscles moving and producing a sound, not the eyes that produce tears or that become dehydrated when forgetting to drink during summer. One does not have a face except for the other, as other. One is othered, while facing the face. It is the impossible staring at you, the ungraspable, the beyond. The episteme is broken precisely because the

311 Emmanuel Levinas, *The Trace of the Other*, p.352.

other, the face of the other as other, remains ungraspable. It is always out of reach while staring at you. The abyss of the void that stands between me and you is the other staring right at you.

Yet there is not a real difference between the I and the face, the observer and the observed, as both are created in the same momentariness of the breaking of the episteme. There isn't anything like an objective observer, observing makes us connected and related to the observed. Perhaps (do you hear Derrida here, the words '*peut-être*' ringing in one's ears?) this is the difficulty that physics is also dealing with, with the coming into being at the moment of the observance. It touches upon that moment that is *real*, that is proto-linguistics, that is behind, before, outside of the worldliness. It is the impossible presenting itself to us, through us, because of usSeeing the other doesn't de-void the void that separates us. The other remains other, even though we try to trick it and tricking ourselves into sensibleness, into reasonableness, intellectual availability. By introducing it to language, to reason, as we have seen, we have lost the other to the present world, it becomes trapped in the structure of time and space. "Not only the world understood by reason ceases to be other, for consciousness finds itself in that world, but everything that is an attitude of consciousness, that is, valorization, feeling, action, labor, and, in general commitment, is in the last analysis self-consciousness, that is, identity and autonomy."[312]

Let us refer back to Levinas here, let us repeat that which has been said, which cannot be said enough, which needs to be repeated, over and over again. The beyond is the One that can never fit in the duality of the other and me. Therefore, the other is me, as it approaches the break, the beyond.

The One in Plotinus is posited beyond being, and also *epekeina nou*. The One of which Plato speaks in the first hypothesis of the

312 Emmanuel Levinas, *The Trace of the Other*, p.346.

Parmenides is foreign to definition and limit, place and time, self-identity and difference with respect to oneself, resemblance and dissemblance, foreign to being and to knowledge – for which all these attributes constitute the categories of knowledge. It is something else than all that, other absolutely and not with respect to some relative term. It is the Unrevealed, but not unrevealed because all knowledge would be too limited or too narrow to receive its light. It is unrevealed because it is One, and because making oneself known implies a duality which already clashes with the unity of the One. The One is not beyond being because it is buried and hidden; it is buried because it is beyond being, wholly other than being.[313]

This other is the One, the only other in the sense of the face, which "emerges as the emblem of everything that fundamentally resists categorization, containment or comprehension."[314] Levinas describes it as being "infinitely foreign"[315], it is the face as "the concrete appearance of the idea of infinity that exists within me."[316] The face of the other is showing me something that I recognise, without referring to something, without making me remember. As such the Other is the most intimate appearance.

Blanchot takes up this Levinassian other as the *autrui*, that other that never becomes someone who fulfils a definite relation to me, a substantive being, a role.[317] Neither does he ascribe the other the status of a God, or something outer-human. Which is why Blanchot refers to this *autrui* as 'indestructible', the essence of human-being that is not within, but always outside, always a longing present in the moment and which is outside our reach, precisely that moment that shows how "for the human being, there is no escaping the human."[318]

313 Emmanuel Levinas, *The Trace of the Other*, p.347.
314 Séan Hand, *Emmanuel Levinas*, p.42.
315 Emmanuel Levinas, *Totality and Infinity*, p.194.
316 Séan Hand, *Emmanuel Levinas*, p.42.
317 See: Maurice Blanchot, *The Infinite Conversation*, p.100.
318 Christopher Fynsk, *Last Steps*, p.46

Only it follows from this that, for me, the Other man who is 'autrui' also risks being always Other than man, close to what cannot be close to me: close to death, close to the night, and certainly as repulsive as anything that comes to me from these regions without horizon. (…) But remember: the Other speaks to me; the decisive interruption of relation speaks precisely as infinite relation in the speech of the Other. (…) When I speak to the Other, the speech that relates me to this other 'accomplishes' and 'measures' that inordinate distance (a distance beyond measure)…[319]

Speech here is not related to words that form discursive spaces. Speech is not language. Speech is that moment that cannot be grasped, like the sound that is heard, but not yet incorporated into knowledge-structures, into epistemic considerations.[320] Speech does not refer, it is outside of writing, it is a call that does precisely that: it calls, calls into being, it calls as becoming. There is a necessity, "…we feel the necessity of the speech. Although we are unable to predict its course, we are possessed by it."[321] There is a touching, a happening of something, an event that does not shape reality, but is devoid of it. It is not the localised happening of being, as Badiou would want us to believe. No, it is much more the becoming human of the beyond before it ever became the animal-human that inhabits the world.

Christopher Fynsk shows that according to Blanchot, "the event *would only have happened* in writing. But it would only have happened had it already happened in a past that is no less 'real' for being immemorial. There has been a touch. (…) The step Blanchot makes (has always made) draws it out as the touch of *autrui.*"[322] Here we find yet another link between the other, the *autrui*, and language. How are we to "understand the saying that occurs in the encounter with *autrui*, and how might we understand a speech that responds to

319 Maurice Blanchot, *The Infinite Conversation*, p.72.
320 Personal conversations with Jim Batcho, 2014.
321 Maurice Merleau-Ponty, *Phenomenology of Perception*, p. 209.
322 Christopher Fynsk, *Language & Relation*, p.244.

the exigency it carries?"[323] As Blanchot elaborates: "There is *the time* of the word, there is the moment that speech begins, lays bare the visage, says the encounter that is this nakedness and says man as the encounter with the extreme and irreducible limit…"[324] Speech is that which calls out the encounter with and because of the Other, which writing can only refer back to, as in the past, as a *having happened*, which it is already incapable of relating to, as any remembering distorts and brings it back into the epistemic relationships.

As such, the other calls forth a responding, an answering. It leaves the human to be a witness of the other, the witness of the moment of becoming-human.

323 Christopher Fynsk, *Last Steps*, p.37.
324 Maurice Blanchot, *The Infinite Conversation*, p.279.

TO WITNESS…

"…language never stands for itself."
~ Hans-Georg Gadamer, *The Relevance of the Beautiful*

We could say that writing is the ultimate witness to the call of the other, the face that we can only face as other. Perhaps it is the only witness, as it is impossible to testify, to give account of that experience except through another means of breaking the boundaries, which can only be done through language, because it was language itself that bound us to our discursive scheme in the first place.

We cannot witness that which lies beyond, we cannot recall it, we cannot linger on it, tell about it, relate it back to the everydayness we call world. And at the same time, we can only be witnesses in the moment of the event, and not beyond that moment. "No witness reports these events; our own consciousness offers no grounds to understand them. Only one document is left to us by them, as silent to the ignorant as it is eloquent to the experienced: language."[325]

When writing this witnessing, when concerned with the reaching of the beyond, this writing "must always also be responsible, in its testimony, for the fact that in such writing *autrui* is at stake."[326] What is important is that for Blanchot, "a language is thus *required*, and whether this required language remains attainable (theoretically, literarily) is the very question of *The Step Not Beyond.*"[327]

Blanchot points to a famous passage in the history of literature, which can be seen as a metaphor for the approach of the impossibility of the other. This is of course the gaze by Orpheus, looking back over his shoulder, trying to connect to his beloved, his desire. And it is this looking, this facing of his beloved that sent Eurydice to the

325 Hermann Usener, as quoted in Giorgio Agamben, *Sacrament of Language*, p.viii.
326 Christopher Fynsk, *Last Steps*, p.135.
327 Christopher Fynsk, *Last Steps*, p.136.

other side of death forever. This look of Orpheus, the looking to the other, is a killing look. By crossing the line, by looking at her face "which is the face of absence" for Blanchot, Orpheus traverses and kills, the moment of the encounter seizes "the presence of Eurydice in the absence of her death."[328]

This desire is always there, it always brings about death. "Orpheus does not signify the eternity and the immutability of the poetic sphere, but, on the contrary, links the 'poetic' to an immeasurable demand that we disappear."[329]

It is Orpheus that reaches for "the furthest art can reach"[330], and it is no wonder that this Other is a woman. Blanchot focuses on Orpheus, how his gaze is necessary, how he could do nothing but then to look. But what about the other, is she only a vehicle for Orpheus to reach out, to leap, to write? Does the other, the woman, only exist for the one who is on the verge of becoming human?

How important is the woman here? Why doesn't Blanchot comment on this: is he afraid and what is he afraid of? He uses the female pronoun cursively many times, to emphasize the otherness of this gender that is ungraspable, unreachable in all aspects, pointing at that which is woman, which is other, but he does not comment. He leaves the woman/other, and gazes upon the one who gazes. How important is it, that it is the man who looks back and therewith foregoes his desire – the woman – but also remains and regains his humanness? By looking he regains his relationship to death and becomes human again. Could a woman ever do this, or can the woman that is always already other, other-ed, ushered-out, uddered, only be already lost, as Blanchot says,[331] into the depth that is the unknown, unreachable, the space she already occupies from the beginning. Can the woman ever be human? Can the truly other ever become real?

328 Christopher Fynsk, *Language & Relation*, p.247.
329 Maurice Blanchot, *Space of Literature*, p.156.
330 Maurice Blanchot, *Space of Literature*, p.171.
331 Maurice Blanchot, *Space of Literature*, p.173.

Are we then to leave the *autrui* for what it is, not comment on it, leave it as a mystery? Is it only when we confine the other to be a mystery that we can continue living our lives in the banality of the world? "Blanchot remarks (...) that only the recognition of the privilege and distance of *autrui* can teach me both what humankind is, and the infinite other that comes to me from the other human being."[332] It is the distance of the other, and specifically the dying other, that "puts me beside myself, this is the only separation that can open me, in its very impossibility, to the Open of a community."[333] Why does Blanchot here invoke an almost Heideggerian formulation? And how is this response of the one towards the other who is dying a relation "in and of language, at the limits of language"?[334]

It is this exposure to something that is beyond-human, which cannot be fathomed by any structure, not by any discourse, not by any episteme. This is the realm of the impossible that escapes the frame. As such, the other, the woman, never becomes. "At this 'human' limit, the address to the other cannot do more or otherwise than stammer a desperate, broken prohibition [the *pas*, but also the 'don't' that is involved with the truly other, the *autrui* (NdB)]. But Blanchot is asserting the community *opens* (which is also to say, communicates) at precisely this limit, where the human opens beyond itself."[335] Human becoming is not merely suffering the neutral. There is always the opening that this suffering of the distance towards the other creates. "We must find in the estrangement of the relation to the other the release of another relation to life from that defined by will, interests, or a reason to live that would assert itself *despite* the knowledge of what is unbearable (suffering, oppression) or the frightening exposure that comes in affliction or anguish."[336]

332 Christopher Fynsk, *Last Steps*, p.41.
333 Maurice Blanchot, *The Unavowable Community*, p.9.
334 Christopher Fynsk, *Last Steps*, p.146.
335 Christopher Fynsk, *Last Steps*, p.150-1
336 Christopher Fynsk, *Last Steps*, p.163.

There we are, back in the frightening space that occupies us from the beginning, whether we are forced into otherness, whether we can face the impossible – that which cannot refer to what is already known. This anguish, this dread, this despair is the result of the human being both, simultaneously, paradoxically. This *other* is both the *other as other* (Levinas) as the *otherness in myself* which is mirroring the other-other, as a distance between the two (Blanchot). What does this mean for becoming? Do we appropriate the other, do we take it and implement it in whatever way we see fit? Do we accustom ourselves to the way we are supposed to think, to act, to write, to observe the other? Can we even let go of this discursive signing, this forceful rendering of reality? Can we be honest to ourselves, to the level of not accepting any thought as our own, always already being said, thought, done, forgetting the distinction between me and the other? Is it possible to both write and be part of *das Man*, forget the authenticity that faces us in becoming human? Can we overcome the framing of the duality that lies enclosed within the observing of the other?

Are we forced to be responsible for the response, to ourselves or to the other? Is every reading already an appropriation that forgoes the essential distinction between the author of the text, and the text itself? There is only text, someone once said, and am I allowed to repeat that, those words, as they appear to me. They appear and speak, and as speech they don't relate anymore to the context they were forced into before. It is me, approaching these words, appropriating, obsessing over them. I do the only thing available to me, the only option open to me. "When Derrida reads Sophocles, Joyce, Kant, Heidegger, Celan, Levinas, Blanchot, or Kafka, he not only accompanies their texts, giving them a second echo, he 'obsesses' them with the theme he is working on, and which thus acts like a photographic developer."[337] Which is why the act is not the same as the person.

337 Anne Dufourmantelle, *Of Hospitality*, p.6.

And if we hear ourselves back, see ourselves from the perspective of the other, we don't recognise it. Is it the other in us, speaking to us? We obsess, can only obsess over the other, the appearance that is always removed from us. "I have NO ideas, only obsessions. Anybody can have ideas. Ideas have never caused anybody's downfall."[338] It is only obsession that can cross the border of the other that I am. It is a touching of the other, the need, the desire to do so, that plunges us into madness.

And then, this other, which is us, which does not escape the discursive space unless we face it, how do we answer to this call to the impossible?

338 Emil Cioran, *On the Heights of Despair*, p.131.

TO ANSWER…

> "To speak in the neutral is to speak at a distance, preserving this distance without mediation and without community, and even in sustaining the infinite distancing of distance…"
> ~ Maurice Blanchot, *The Infinite Conversation*

This responding to the other, in which the other embodies our desire, through which the other lets us become human, is facing the other as an answering.

When, for example, Simone Weil says simply, 'Human life is impossible. But misfortune alone makes this felt,' we understand very well that it is not a question of denouncing the unbearable or the absurd character of life — negative determinations that belong to the realm of possibility — but of recognizing in impossibility our most human belonging to immediate human life, the life that it falls to us to sustain each time that, stripped through misfortune of the clothed forms of power, we reach the nakedness of every relation: that is to say, the relation to naked presence, the presence of the other, and in the infinite passion that comes from it. In the same way, Simone Weil writes: 'Desire is impossible.' And now we understand that desire is precisely this relation to impossibility, that it is impossibility become relation— separation itself, in its absolute — that becomes alluring and takes form.[339]

But what does it lead to, this desire that is the impossible? How is our relation to naked presence forming our being?

We still face the question of the desire that marks the framed relation to the impossible, and the answer that is pre-dictated by it, because of the nature of questioning. We ask the question of the other, and expect nothing less than an answer that does not by itself refer to something specific. So let us begin, once again. To explore this

339 Maurice Blanchot, *The Infinite Conversation*, p.47.

answering as a becoming human, answering to, answering for the other, let us trace again those comprehensions that will lead us astray, bringing up the usual suspects: Blanchot, Levinas and Derrida. For no other reason than to focus, perhaps and except for the fact that it is only men. Perhaps, maybe, this manning-up will let us approach this other in a responsive manner, that leaves nothing to the will of the subject, to the rational being that is of the animal-human we have been taught to be, that we always already are forced to be.

Blanchot, that defender of death, that hermit from the south of France, talks about an answering to (*répondre de*), "bringing me to respond – without responsibility – for this relation in the most passive passion (relation with the non-concerning) which I neither suffer nor assume."[340] It is the responding to the beyond, without having the ability to, for which any mentioning is already a foresaking. It is not taking on this responding that makes one human; the answering lies in the responding itself, precisely in the face of its failure, its impossibility. The aporia, that "undecidable crossing of the ways"[341] needs to be taken in, accepted as the wholly unknown. It is that moment where thought begins. "Thought is in essence a force of mastery. It is continually bringing the unknown back to the known, breaking up its mystery to possess it, shed light on it. Name it."[342] And in naming it, bringing it back under the force of the present, the epistemic space that makes us have to start longing, the reaching for the impossible starts at the beginning again.

Levinas, friend of Blanchot, what do you have to say? Is there an opening that is not already included in Blanchot? Is his movement away from the neutral, to include the radicality of the Other as other, a re-stating of the same? Is his ethical response to that which cannot be witnessed, an inclusion of what for Blanchot is the neutral, the other, the *au-delà*, that cannot and should always be taken on one's

340 Maurice Blanchot, *The Step Not Beyond*, p.123.
341 Anne Dufourmantelle, *Of Hospitality*, p.26.
342 Anne Dufourmantelle, *Of Hospitality*, p.28.

shoulders? Or is Levinas trying to break away from the fear of the *other-as-other*, and does he embrace philosophy as a non-knowing of being, not being occupied with the philosophical allergy of leaving the other precisely the other. Levinas wants to fight this being-indifferent towards the other.[343]

The other is a commandment, not an answering but "an inescapable order (…) which puts an end to the detachment of consciousness."[344] The countenance, the face in which the other remains the other, "unsaddles the intentionality which aims at it."[345] The Self which relates to the other, which answers to it, faces it, is the "Idea of the Infinite", which is desire. There is no way to get out of the paradox that talks, repeats, excavates this internal relation of this original desire for the impossible, with the idea of the beyond that is out of reach. The infinite that cannot be fathomed, no matter which calculus we develop. "It consists, paradoxically, in thinking more than is thought; while yet conserving its immeasurability in correspondence with thought, to enter into relation with what cannot be taken hold of, while fully guaranteeing its cannot-be-taken-hold-of status."[346]

But when I, myself, approach this other, to ask for forgiveness, to plead for an acceptance, a being seen, being in a relation with that which is who is me, then it is the radical Other that hears me.

"God is, in a sense, the *other, par excellence*, the other as other, the absolutely other – and nonetheless my standing with this God depends only upon myself."[347] It is me who decides how and whether to approach the other as other. Although Levinas remarks that my neighbour is even more removed from my Self, as my neighbour can withdraw his face, my neighbour has to accept my appeasement, whereas God-as-Other cannot but pardon me, whenever I beseech Him.

343 Emmanuel Levinas, *On the Trail of the Other*, p.36.
344 Emmanuel Levinas, *On the Trail of the Other*, p.41.
345 Emmanuel Levinas, *On the Trail of the Other*. p.41.
346 Emmanuel Levinas, *On the Trail of the Other*, p.42.
347 Emmanuel Levinas, *Nine Talmudic Readings*, p.16.

Derrida needs to step in here. To safe the face from religious dogmas that we so easily fall into once the G-word has been mentioned. Notice the amount of hairs on your back that stand up straight once we utter the ultimate other, once we dare name that Name that needs to remain unsaid for us to not lose our faith. What are we afraid of? What makes this *aporia* closed off, what makes us stop connecting once it has been named? Does the Name destroy our attempts to reach for it? Are we afraid of telling ourselves one more bedtime story that will get us to sleep, but from which we will never be able to awake again without destroying everything that we thought we achieved?

So, let us not name it. Let us know the name, and forget about it. Knowing would condemn us to understand, would frame it. Naming is framing. Let's recast this die, this all-encompassing Other that is always already implied in every word that does not conform, that does not create a reference that is pure – which is wordless, every linguistic operation since the catastrophe surrounding the Tower of Babel. As Benjamin confirms, "[t]hings have no proper names except in God."[348] Building that tower from scratch, without knowing anything but our desire to build, that moment that we took for granted that our discourse and episteme were congruent, overlapped and created the world itself. We were the masters over our understanding, so we took the Name of God-as-creator-not-yet-Other upon ourselves.[349] And we fell. I continue to fall, as all children fall down, when and once they realise for the first time that they are utterly alone, that their cries are meaningless, that their mother cannot but respond, but that it is only to clear her consciousness, not the child's pain. This is ethics today, always only related to the Self, devoid of communion with the other, precisely because we know that this other-as-God is not here, is beyond, is dead.Or are we then again within the realm we are meant to escape? But it is my space, the

348 Walter Benjamin, *Early Writings*, p.265.
349 See: Walter Benjamin, *Early Writings*, p.264-5.

space created and creating the Western *world*, it is the essence of that which is only a repetition of the Same. So let us retrace our steps, go back to this original waiting that leaves open what can be received. Which is what Derrida opens up for us, when he discusses hospitality. The openness towards that which is fully other, that *Xenia*, needs to be received. We cannot demand it to speak our language, it can refrain from giving us its name, it can demand even the daughters of the house for personal use. This is what openness to the other is, to not limit its appearance and its reception on the basis of one's own ethical dispositions. "An act of hospitality can only be poetic."[350]

Hospitality is part of the question itself, the question of naming that which is beyond naming. "In these regions, we rediscover the open question of the relationship between hospitality and the question, in other words of a hospitality beginning with the name, the question of the name else opening up without question…"[351] The responding to the question of the other, the desire for the impossible, is an opening towards the other as if she were myself, ready to face the gravest consequences, giving up all our claims to our own being and our home – this is hospitality. Not a sharing, but a radical giving that cannot be undone. The gift of death.

Where have we wandered? Perhaps these are the wrong men to ask. Perhaps. Except. Should we turn to George Bataille, as he understands that experience itself is the posing of the question, full of fever and anxiety, of what a man knows, needs to know, should know, to construct being.[352] Perhaps we turn again to Hannah Arendt, as she knew very well how "[s]peaking and acting people differentiate each other actively from each other, instead of being empty and differentiated; these are the way, within which man reveals himself."[353]

---

350 Jacques Derrida, *Of Hospitality*, p.3.
351 Anne Dufourmantelle, *Of Hospitality*, p.12 & 14.
352 Georges Bataille, *L'expérience intérieure*, p.16.
353 Hannah Arendt, *Vita Activa oder Vom tätigen Leben*, p.214.

Or should we turn to that man that cannot be left out of any true discussion of matters concerning experience and being, the fourfold and the gods? Martin Heidegger. Are we merely repeating his thinking all along? Is it the notion of *Mit-sein* as part of *being-in-the-world* authentically all that is at issue here?

Let us back up. Forget the names, the tropes, the authority that is implied in a thinking that is posited rather than thought through. How do we understand this *respond-ere*, this answering to the other as a beginning of being human? Why is this the human reaching for the beyond, this human becoming, that is exactly the failing of the responding to the other that is us? And what happens at that moment, the precise present that can never referred back to, which never leaves the present, and can only be repeated. It is conversion, the moment of possession. The moment of madness.

CONVERSION – TOUCHING

"Ich fragte: seit wann ist die Stadt erbaut?
Wohin ist Wald und Meer und Schalmei?
Sie schrien, und hörten nicht mein Wort:
So ging es ewig an diesem Ort,
Und wird so gehen ewig fort.
Und aber nach fünfhundert Jahren
Will ich desselbigen Weges fahren."
~ Friedrich Rückert, *Chidher*

Conversion is that radical change back and through language. Let me converse, approach the other in me, move away from the known, and change directions. Conversion is that radical change that exchanges, the positive for the negative, the negative for the positive. The conversion rate of change is zero to one. Everything that was possible, becomes beyond reach, it is too obvious to be taken up again, it only produces vomit. Instead we remain in the realm of the impossible, touching the darkness as it comes our way. It becomes our way, it is our way. We matter only insofar we are that other that limits and traces our self. We converse, are conversed, we are in relation to that which can never behold the relation. It is the reversal of it all, that we consider conversion.[354]

We are not to control the impossible, but we merely desire to reach it. The epistemic structures are always already there and whenever we actively break them, we only once more install them, follow them, wish them into existence. Therefore, we need something from the beyond itself, the *aporia*, the void, to fill us. "In general, we must not wish for the disappearance of any of our troubles, but the grace to transform them."[355]

354 Simone Weil, *Grace and Gravity*, p.35.
355 Simone Weil, *Grace and Gravity*, p.35.

It is the cry for the other without attaining it, but instead renouncing all that we already have, that converges us into a continual conversing. "We only possess what we renounce; what we do not renounce escapes from us. In this sense, we cannot possess anything whatsoever unless it passes through God."[356] God, that instigator, that detonator, the designator of the impossible which is only there when not expected.

It is the friend that comes in the guise of the stranger, that can only be accepted to come inside, given hospitality *before* it is named, framed, distinguished from her stranger-ness. Why do we always need to know where someone is from, whenever we approach someone? Her otherness is denied by turning to her roots, by giving her a background from which she emerges. The other that we are ourselves, needs the open space, the total void that is given to us by the *aporia* itself, in order for her to truly come to us. This opening to the other without limiting it to the possible, is the religious moment.

Blanchot talks about this, when he refers to the experience of Simone Weil at the age of 29, as to when she experienced the other.

And the word conversion is not a word she uses willingly, except in the sense of this word that she finds in the texts of Plato. The violence of a decisive turnabout, a capital break, are instead events to be mistrusted because of the illusory hopes their vividness cannot fail to bring forth, just as seeking God and finding God are unsuitable expressions, which, at the most, indicate that we have found a false God and that in seeking have forgotten what cannot be sought. Conversion cannot but be silent, invisible, perfectly secret; it requires of the one in whom it is accomplished only the same attention and the same immobility to which it was the brief, illuminating response.[357]

356 Simone Weil, *Grace and Gravity*, p.34.
357 Maurice Blanchot, *The Infinite Conversation*, p.107.

It is the most intimate, the personal response of the human-becoming to the other which presents its face. Which is why the other as the sign of the impossible, that we harbour within ourselves at all times, is the secret that moves us. And here we find ourselves far removed from the radical break that Badiou talks about, formally and clean, which for him is a violent breaking without accepting the impossible *as* impossible.

Instead we move about, converting our convergence, being with-the-edge, to-the-edge, the rim, the rod, the shoot, the stick. The leaning towards the male member, that which is always other, othering the truly other, and putting it down, bringing it down. Touching the other is that breaking that takes place without extending past the moment, the present, the now. It does not shape either the one or the other, it creates a connection that goes beyond the physical. Just like it is not the eyes that watch, just like it is the shapes of the momentary that are beyond controlling, beyond understanding. And because of its secretive nature, unknown, unmentionable even to ourselves, giving examples is a dis-grace.

Conversion is the moment that one is put under, down under, at the other side of the world, in the excessive moment that is created by language. We dwell in these voids that are left whenever we trace back towards that other that inhabits our space, our heart. It is the darkness that is left outside of the realm of language, that cannot be approached, touched, maintained unless we submit our desire, when we acknowledge that our meeting of the other that is us, has left us possessed. It is that possession that again frames and forces us to submit to the rule of the known. "This nocturnal side of speech could be called obsession."[358] Which also according to Cioran is the only way to matter, to be living in the face of meaninglessness that frames us, that surrounds our existence.

358 Anne Dufourmantelle, *Of Hospitality*, p.3.

This obsessive breaking, the stepping beyond the epistemic worldliness, also means that we can no longer dwell in a space. We become homeless. We are not on our way to language and have now definitely said goodbye to Heidegger. We interrupt this dwelling of the always-already, of the being in language, in the frame of the cave-dweller. We dwell unrelated, in such a manner that "only the nomadic affirmation *remains*."[359] The dwelling is no longer related to our belonging somewhere, we are no longer part of the world we inhabit, we let go of these connotations, these places that we have always already found ourselves in. We might feel connected to our surrounding, and we are connected, we always are, but this no longer defines our being, our humanness is precisely confirmed by this letting go. It is the human-animal and the animal itself that is moved by its need to belong, to eat, to be part and subjected to his environment. As such the human-animal is only, exists only, is being only insofar as he is connected to this environment.

Once we touch the beyond, once we touch the other, we not only become human-human, we also leave the space that is created for us, by us, as we are thrown into the world. We leave the epistemic space that we occupy. We say *no* to occupation, the occupying of our bodies as the manner of identifying ourselves. And once we touch, once we violent tear away from the spaces that define us, we lose that which was formerly known as ourselves. We become the mad figure that is beyond knowing, beyond understanding, as the relation to space – and time for that matter – has been disrupted.

Let us explore this, that violence and madness which surrounds the conversion, the religious. It is all that matters, for the rest is a mere dwelling that encroaches upon us.

---

359 Maurice Blanchot, *The Step Not Beyond*, p.33.

VIOLENCE

"The possible, so it seems, exists at the limits of the impossible."
~ Georges Bataille, *Unfinished System of Nonknowledge*

This longing for the beyond must eventually lead somewhere – to a failure, or an attainment. The *other* cannot be forever removed; it is impossible, it is facing us and entertaining us, it is driving us mad as it calls upon us. We must do something. It is death that cannot be faced except in our solitude; and precisely because we know this, feel this in our bones and accept this when we first realise our beloved cat hides below the porch to die by itself, it is from that moment on that we fight this realising. We scratch our faces, we tear out our hair, we cut ourselves if only we can for a moment forget this ultimate loneliness.

We become our own death-makers. Violence awaits, there is nothing else to be done, but to stop this essential truth from entering our sphere or reality. And the other, with his face facing us, reminds us of this void that divides us. All day. Everyday. Even when we are alone, we face our own other that lives within us, that creates the image we have of ourselves. The other living in us, makes us lonelier than ever. As Blanchot murmurs, "we must recall … that in the exposure of *autrui*, violence always awaits…"[360]

Are we to be afraid of this violence? Is our movement away from it, our response to the other, only a fear of the other's violence that makes the beginning of our continuing to be both beyond and simultaneously accepting everything we are not and can never be? Is violence, the war that rages in us, always to be covered by what is seen as womanliness, of the soft love that covers our wounds, that tries to heal the gaps that come about when meeting the other?

360 Christopher Fynsk, *Last Steps*, p.52.

No! The woman itself is the violent figure that is responding to the figure she is made out to be — not to destroy who she is through violence, but always violently opposing the destruction of the otherness that she embodies. She births the other, always. As was already known in Tao and Buddhism, the woman has endless energy in order to create, to birth, to reproduce, whereas the man is characterized by a limiting in order to accomplish the already possible. The woman's mood swings are only connected to the failure of this birthing, the inaccessibility to what she needs in order to create the other. And if she does, when she births that other, it is taken instantaneously as an object of the world, it is labelled, named, numbered, wrapped in the warmth of the first-person-singular that is always male. The destruction of the relation of the mother-birther and the other she is internally connected to, is – in this Western world – done by the male, the dominator who appropriates everything that she produced, marking it as his own. It is the man who gives his names, his genes, his money. He claims the right to be maker, creator, by linking existence to the realm of language. By naming it, framing it, bringing it into the epistemical realm, he brings the being from beyond into the naivety of the possible. He forgets the body from which everything originates, from which the beyond violently imposes itself into the present, and takes that place by unplacing, unspacing the other. He tries to overcome the violence that leaves him speechless, tries to forget it, leave it in the darkness below the blanket. The mother may raise the other, feed it, carry the burden on her back, until the *other* is recognised as human-animal-being, functions independently, and is part of the male linguistic society. It is then that the violence starts in full speed, instituting actualised situations of framing into sameness, in places like school that bring the *other* en masse together as groups of citizens, installing state-infused illusionary ideas of individualism that make the other part of the Same, once and for all.

How can we accept the violence that is involved in revolving around the otherness that is ourselves? How do we face, implement, bring about the acceptance of the *impossible as impossible*, not making it actual, but taking it in, as the pill of the future that will instantly kill you if you approach it, this impossible that brings death to the immediate surface? The acceptance of the failure is the radical violence that kills instantaneously, brings to an end our relationship with the world that we are already facing to an immediate end. The world that tries to bring us into being by destroying our otherness. It does not face us, let us not face others, but masks our true otherness in slogans and forges us into telephone numbers.[361]

But let us not fall into the trap of saying *no* to everything, as our experience of the void that the face of our own otherness faces is fundamentally a saying *yes*.

Yes, impossible.

Yes, life.

The yes is the most violent thing we can do in life. It is the *saying no* that Nietzsche was talking about, only in the positive, embracing sense that declares our otherness without trying to understand it, without making it into an existence.

We live in a world in which failure and the letting something that is other and unactualised cannot even be expressed in language in a manner that is not connected in a non-relation. Language always already makes it into a presence; it is the word that lets the real come in, that makes it into an actual that denies anything that is beyond, on the other side. The river that divides the city cannot be bridged; one has to accept the failure of the rope being thrown to the other side; the violence with which the water that comes up will splash the citizens on each side, who wonder what it is and by doing so deny the existence of the overcoming. Any attempt to understand,

361 See: Giorgio Agamben, *Infancy and History.*

to know how and why it becomes, is a letting in of reality as it exists. The denying of this all-encompassing world from which there is no escape, is the violence of the mother. A violence that cannot be called violence, as it creates. Yet it destroys the sanity that might still surround us, as we have come to the point that the letting in of the other is accepted as the failure and the beginning of becoming human-human, ourselves.

We need to face this lack, this potency of failure — positively. Without without, with with. Everything in the epistemological space trembles in front of this possibility of the impossible, and forces us to relate back again to the world that we live in. It makes us think there is only connectedness to the realm of the discourse — and let us call this potency, knowledge, truth, if you will. But this is a success, whereas we're facing a need to fail. "Potency – or knowledge — is the specifically human faculty of connectedness as lack; and language, in its split between language and speech, structurally contains this connectedness, is nothing other than this connectedness."[362]

It is a violence related to language and to the fear of being appropriated by it… "that space of the unknowable that the speech apprehends and before which it stops us short for a moment, scared."[363] But this being scared is only another way of being sacred. Crossing the line, moving from the profane to the profound, we become what is a 'sacred' being. We can no longer be violated, the act of moving out of what cannot be left, leaves us as the untouchable. We have become sacred beings, those who save the city, the world, those who sacrificed their mental states of belonging to the world, who have left the realm of the accepted, the rational.

362 Giorgio Agamben, *Infancy and History*, p.7.
363 Anne Dufourmantelle, *Of Hospitality*, p.24.

But leaving the realm of the accepted, forces us into the abject, the monstrous. "What is abject, (…), the jettisoned object, is radically excluded and draws me towards the radical place where meaning collapses."[364] It is the radical break with the known, the clean, the proper. At its moment of abjection, that may perhaps never be anything beyond that moment, it is untouchable, sacred.

"Essentially different from 'uncanniness', more violent, too, abjection is elaborated through a failure to recognize its kin; nothing is familiar, not even the shadow of a memory."[365] Which is also why our desire cannot be identified, nor lead us to this monstrous outside, this facing of the other that is ourselves. Desire is always related to objects, whereas we need to leave the realm of objects and subjects. All dichotomies only ground us once more, leave us possessed, possessive. The monsters are those that are unrelatable.

But this abject is important as it points us towards the "the artistic experience, which is rooted in the abject it utters and by the same token purifies, appears as the essential component of religiosity."[366] It is the sacred that comes into play, that which cannot be touched or brought back into the mundane. The abject is the violent break which brings us into relation with the other that inhabits me. And being obsessed by the other, with the other, which violently brings me to break away with the identity which relates me to the possible present that is familiar, I am left hopelessly de-void, left alone with the ultimate void. I become human at the expense of myself. I become mad. "The madman is not, strictly speaking, a person: he is *no one*, a blank, an empty speech receptacle."[367]

364 Julia Kristeva, *Powers of Horror*, p.2.
365 Julia Kristeva, *Powers of Horror*, p.5.
366 Julia Kristeva, *Powers of Horror*, p.1.
367 Shoshana Felman, *Writing and Madness*, p.110.

MADNESS

> "At the edge of life you feel you are no longer master of the life within you, that subjectivity is an illusion, and that uncontrollable forces are seething inside you, evolving with no relation to a personal center or a definite, individual rhythm."
> ~ Emil Cioran, *On the Heights of Despair*

What are we to write, then? Are we in possession of a power that is driving us, leading us towards that place which is out of reach? Is there a talent, a specific humanness that is behind it, is it a conspiracy of reality, that epistemic bastard that makes us believe in what is always already the case? And what are words doing with us — are we there to succumb, to fall prey to the forces that inhabit them, and inhibit us? Are we to become pragmatists, realists that take into account what works and base their worldview on it? How are we to face our desire that creeps in our everyday life, whenever we face a poem that is not in the realist plane, that moves something in us that is seemingly only muscles and bonWe write. Which is to say, we are mad, going mad, becoming mad, dwelling in the realm that is labelled *other*, autrui, mad. Which is to say, we become woman, that one that is always already other, other-ed. But she is not woman in response to the one that is, not in comparison with those she needs to relate to. She might be all that, not-man, daughter-of, mother-of, sister-of, wife-of, girlfriend-of, slave-of. But this is not what makes us, her, other. If this is all there is, then there is no construction of the Self outside of the hermeneutical space.

But why is this madness? Are we to follow Foucault's definition of madness, primarily, as "a lack of language, an 'absence of production', the silence of stifled, repressed language?"[368] This absence of production, *l'absense d'oeuvre*,[369] is the absence of the work, the com-

368 Shoshana Felman, *Writing and Madness*, p.14.
369 Michel Foucault, *Histoire de Folie*, Preface.

plete work that is produced, that forms the epistemic structure of the author, the one who writes, who dwells in the realms of language, of speech, of literature. Madness is the absence of that, precisely that which creates it. It is a failure, a reaching of the absence that must, in order to even be reckoned with, already be part of what it.

Is madness a failure in translation? Is it a bringing to language of what lies beyond? "To speak about madness is to speak about the difference between languages: to import into one language the strangeness of another; to unsettle the decisions language has prescribed to us so that, somewhere between languages, will emerge the freedom to speak."[370] But what is this freedom, what is speech if not merely another failure to put the madness into linguistic frames once again? "How can madness, in itself, survive translation into language?"[371]

Is madness not itself a questionable term? Is it defined by the epistemic realm that pushes it to the limit, places it at that moment in which behaviour, speech, being of the one who is deemed mad no longer belongs to the what-is? Can it ever be, that the mad person is designated as such by those who linger in the possible, the world? The mad are forever banned from the world. They are pushed out, pushed aside, taken out of the equilibrium which is called reality. Whether they are locked up, killed or denied, they remain ostracised. They do not belong to that which is part of the law. Which is why madness does not make someone receive a softer judgement. No, "madness wipes out the crime."[372]

It is reasonableness itself that creates it, delineates it, as "madness is essentially a phenomenon of thought, of thought which claims to denounce, in another's thought, the other of thought: that which thought is not."[373] Thought, madness. Writing, speaking, we leave the realm of the sayable in order to un-say, to overcome the borders of

370 Shoshana Felman, *Writing and Madness*, p.19.
371 Shoshana Felman, *Writing and Madness*, p.66.
372 Michel Foucault, *Abnormal*, p.31.
373 Shoshana Felman, *Writing and Madness*, p.36.

thought as such. Which we cannot. Because we are strewn into the realm which is always already imposed, which is looking down on us precisely because it is ourselves doing the looking, framing.

It is the ability of self-reflection, which — according to Hegel — is why man "has the privilege of madness"[374]. It is self-reflection, the looking from within the world we find ourselves in towards otherness. It is the computer program, programmed to program itself. It creates a loop, an error, a failure, as the paradox of being inside and creating oneself is turned into a breaking of ontological space that never happens: madness. We are thus to understand Pascal, who said these famous overly used and misused, taken and appropriated words, and which therefore are to remain without origin: "Men are so necessarily mad that not to be mad would only be another form of madness." Are we truly using his words here, or are we referring to what speaks through them to us? Are we to understand anything from that beyond that is other, that is captured by the words, the language of the other? Or are we misusing and misappropriating right from the start?

Is it this misappropriation of thought which was hailed forth by Descartes that we need to un-do? Descartes said: "I who am thinking cannot be mad."[375] Are we then to give up on thinking once we acknowledge our desire for the impossible, our longing for the breaking of the possible reasonableness that forms the epistemic grounding of our world? Is it the limit of thinking we are after here, or did the pronouncement of Descartes, enabling us to decree the separation of thinking and madness, set us up for our original failure?

Are we always comprehending comprehension as a limiting, which encloses us and confines ourselves to this thinking, this world, this epistemic realm? "How can we comprehend without objectify-

374 Georg W. Hegel, "Philosophie de l'esprit" in: *Encyclopédie*, p.383.
375 See: Michel Foucault, *Histore de Folie*, p.58.

ing, without excluding?"[376] The task is doubly impossible, according to Foucault. "The perception which seeks to seize them in their natural state belongs necessarily to a world which has already captured them. The freedom of madness can only be heard from the top of the fortress which holds it prisoner."[377]

According to Derrida, it is not Descartes' *cogito*, the thinking that excludes madness, but the framing into language, the *speaking* that excludes, that dismisses madness.[378] It is the letting go of meaning which is madness; and, as such, it is opposed to the mastering of reason. Which is why the movement of the reaching beyond the possible is doubly mad: firstly, because it is impossible – reasonableness dictates that one does not do anything impossible; secondly, because it is the search for that realm that not only lies beyond meaning, beyond the epistemic, beyond the truth-beholding, but which is a realm that is not related to anything which contains meaning. It is acceptance of the radicality of the demand of the impossible which leads us towards madness itself.

Do we repeat the Nietzschean Dionysian movement? Are we to see the breaking of the rational, this movement of chaos, of being a stranger, as opposed to *logos*? No. This breaking might be purely un-rational, but it is not a-rational, not devoid of reason. It is precisely because of the rational, the structures, that it comes about. The outside-of-*logos* accepts that there is a relation to the limit that is part of the rational domain. We only need to remind ourselves of what Cioran mentions: that madness always follows or is followed by the lucidity of reason. "The premonition of madness is complicated by the fear of *lucidity* in madness, the fear of the moments of return and reunion, when the intuition of disaster is so painful that it almost provokes a greater madness."[379] If it weren't for the lucidity,

376 Shoshana Felman, *Writing and Madness*, p.56.
377 Michel Foucault, *Histoire de Folie*, Preface.
378 See: Jacques Derrida, *L'Ecriture et la différance*, p.84.
379 Emil Cioran, *On the Heights of Despair*, p.38.

the relation that always remains, that always binds us to the rational, madness would be a pure experience of the other.

Perhaps it is not strange for philosophy to have always shied away from the un-rational, the bodily existence of the human, philosophically. The opposition that is supposed to be present, the mind-body, the emotion versus rational, the male-female distinction, is all illusionary. As Dufourmantelle explains, it is a risky business to challenge this mistrust of emotion, of the non-rational, the non-sensical. Yet "[e]motion is the signature of alterity. It is a sign, precisely, that there is otherness, and that the other in question is reaching us."[380] To this we need to add, that it is not even a specific 'other in question' that is reaching us, it is the other in itself, even the other that is me, that is reaching for a connection to the rational. Failing, just as the rational fails to embrace the non-sensical. And so we repeat.

Madness, then, is the acceptance of this paradox, this schizophrenic state of the double in me. The other that others me, that brings me into trouble, that makes me forget the reality that is implied in every thought I think, in every word I utter. Madness is un-philosophical in that it doesn't block out the other, doesn't reframe the understanding of reality. Madness lies in the experience, the momentary of the forgetfulness of time. Madness is therefore purely sexual. Perhaps madness invokes the letting go of the frontiers of philosophy, and instead fights the true and only battle in the area of the self that is split between being as a pre-structured self, an ontological shape that is knowable under the right circumstances, and a self that is always outside the reach of the known. This madness, this accepting, is what moves us. It is what violates everything, which destroys and leaves nothing untouched. The mad person (if we can talk about it being a person in the first place) is the child that puts everything in its mouth, without knowing why, but feels compelled out of sheer want to experience to become.

380 Anne Dufourmantelle, *Blind Date*, p.21.

CONCLUDING THE BREAK

> "If I can invent what I invent, if I have the ability to invent what I invent, that means that the invention follows a potentiality, an ability that is in me, and thus it brings nothing new. It does not constitute an event."
> ~ Jacques Derrida, *A Certain Impossible Possibility of Saying the Event*

In the end, the question remains, as to whether fundamental rupture of the episteme is possible. Is it useless to try to think about that what is impossible, beyond, precisely because of its structure which limits the beyond of what we are able to think or conceive of? Usefulness is not something philosophy can ever ascertain. But, the real question, what it means for human beings to have this focus on the issue of 'change', of this attainment of the impossible, is what concerns us here.

The reaching of the other, the beyond, the impossible, is a radical move, that introduces a new while continuing to stay the same. "A work conceived radically is a movement of the same unto the other which never returns to the same"[381], as Levinas puts it. This is a fundamental impossibility, not an historical accident – as it is not based upon contingent factors, but claims the grounding of questioning and language itself.

For Blanchot it seems all too simple, the overcoming of the paradox. Is he not touched by the despair? Is there for him really a way out of the entanglement of life that is most eloquently shown by the structuring of language itself? Blanchot acknowledges the violence, the painful element that lies at the heart of the speaking of, and through, and to, the other that is *autrui*, but he seems unaware that this is not just a pain that accompanies man as he proceeds through

381 Emmanuel Levinas, *The Trace of the Other*, p.348.

life. It is at once the despair that gives life and takes it away by blocking the possibility of attaining the impossible. "I am: therefore the world is meaningless."[382] It is the beginning of nihilism and the end of all meaning. Where does the hopefulness come from that accompanies the continuous struggle to move towards the beyond? Why is it that the mystic experience keeps elevating this despair and brings us to taking another step, even though we know it's the last step we will ever be taking?

Describing the *becoming* human, the *human* becoming, does not signify the eventuality of this becoming. I must agree with Heidegger that only through our despair, through our primordial relationship to our *Verfallenheit* in the everyday-ness which is the possible, which is the discursive space we find ourselves in, that only through this despairing relation, can we ever encounter the other as other. Once we forget this despair, this emotional state of paradox that entrenches us, that inhibits us to take action, the other can never even show itself as other.

It is in this specific place that we always need to place our reaching for the impossible. Not outside of this condition. It is this condition of facing the desire that we can first of all become human, recognise the human in and as the other. Even though language might start from the moment of reaching the beyond,[383] that moment in which the impossible is approached, there is always already something before that. The other has at that moment already shown her Face. The moment of human becoming thus lies before language. Language appropriates this becoming, voices it, shapes it, brings it back to the realm of the what-is. This is why the problem of language is always limited, always of secondary importance. Language is not a meaning-giving, but an invocation. Not a comprehension, but a shape, a visible form of the relation towards the other.

382 Emil Cioran, *On the Heights of Despair*, p.31.
383 See: Levinas, *Totality and Infinity.*

So, what is this facing of the impossible? "You change, you live the non-change as the trace and the mark of that which, not concerning, could not change you."[384] Which is to say, according to Fynsk: "to bring to all existing the trace of alterity, therefore, to change by *living* nonchange as a writing of the relation to something that does not concern the interests of life in the world."[385] This concerns not merely a specific relation to the beyond, the impossible. More than that, it is "the first step of a conversation that releases the possibility of an infinite, absolute relation to what concerns in life".[386]

This is the last step that can be taken. At least according to Blanchot, to Fynsk. What does this step look like? Fynsk calls it the 'exilic step'. It is the step that interrupts the epistemic worldliness. It is an entering into some form of silence, as a place outside. In the words of Blanchot: "If [these interruptions] occurred in such a way that you should once have to be silent, you would never again be able to speak of them."[387] This step as an interruption must "be understood as a *refusal* of the all-embracing law of discourse."[388] It is not a denial, it is a refusal, as it acknowledges the limit it is breaking.

What is interesting to note is how, for Blanchot, the act of writing, or perhaps better to say, the possibility of writing, "would have to occur in a region *separate* from the order of discourse, though it would not fail to 'touch' and displace, while leaving 'intact', the concepts of 'truth', 'unity', and 'subject' presupposed in this discursive regime."[389] This so-called discursive regime is the epistemic framework within which all discourses take place. Is then the act of writing for Blanchot merely a breaking open of the language, the discourse, within one finds oneself? Is he aware of the further impossibility of breaking with the underlying episteme; is he being humbled here

384 Maurice Blacnhot, *The Infinite Conversation*, p.xxiv.
385 Christopher Fynsk, *Last Steps*, p.104.
386 Christopher Fynsk, *Last Steps*, p.104.
387 Maurice Blanchot, *The Infinite Conversation*, p.xxii.
388 Christopher Fynsk, *Last Steps*, p.105.
389 Christopher Fynsk, *Last Steps*, p.140.

while facing the episteme? Or is Blanchot simply not making the distinction between the epistemic reality and the discursive realm? Is the breaking of language, through language, the possibility which is presented by writing as a conversation between myself and the radical other, the breaking of the epistemic regime that informs the discursive, the law that envelops all?

Writing is the utmost form of madness, especially when it is acknowledged that one needs to lose all ground, even lose language itself, and thereby one's own identity, one's relation to the world, whenever the pen hits the paper. This madness, that is violently distorted by the lucidity of the real that breaks through after each moment has passed, at the moment the writing is being done. I am distracted by the world that I am trying to flee from, but the despair that makes me write also attaches me to this world and makes me part of the realm that I can never occupy while writing.

We fail, each moment in time — which presents itself each moment we break away from time altogether. Writing madness is impossible.

So, we are deeply rooted in the philosophy of difference, as Deleuze describes it. By recognising the other as other, we find a difference internal to the Idea: affirmative, categorical, dynamic.[390] Which is why the other, or the impossible for that matter, is never attained. By applying the mechanism of repetition, by the act of playing, enacted instead of being known, as the impossible can never belong to the realm of the knowable known, the epistemic space.[391] "The variations express, rather, the differential mechanisms which belong to the essence and the origin of that which is repeated."[392]

390 Gilles Deleuze, *Difference & Repetition*, p.24.
391 See: Gilles Deleuze, *Difference & Repetition*, p.14.
392 Gilles Deleuze, *Difference & Repetition*, p.17.

Or, as Derrida already told us, which we can only keep repeating:

> Similarly, when you conduct an epistemological analysis or an analysis in the history of science and technology, you examine a field in which a theoretical, mathematical, or technological invention is possible, a field that may be called a paradigm in one case, an episteme in another, or yet again a configuration; now, if the structure of the field makes an invention possible (at a given point in time a given architectural invention is possible because the state of society, architectural history, and architectural theory make it possible), then this invention is not an invention. Precisely because it's possible. It merely develops and unfolds a possibility, a potentiality that is already present and therefore it is not an event. For there to be an invention event, the invention must appear impossible. What was not possible becomes possible. In other words, the only invention possible is the invention of the impossible. This statement may seem to be a game, a mere rhetorical contradiction. In fact, I believe it is an irreducible necessity. If there is invention — and maybe there never is, just as there may never be giving or forgiving — but if there is invention, it's possible only on the condition of being impossible. The event's eventfulness depends on this experience of the impossible. What comes to pass, as an event, can only come to pass if it's impossible. If it's possible, if it's foreseeable, then it doesn't come to pass.[393]

Should we end here, with the voice of an-other? Or is it me who is the other, rupturing my own discourse as I move along, failing but attempting? Am I to testify to my own madness? Or is it you, my dear other?

393 Jacques Derrida, *A Certain Impossible Possibility*, p.450-51.

conclusion

"The Way that can be articulately described,
is not the Unchanging Way."
~ Lao Tzu, *Tao Te Ching*

THE MADNESS OF CONCLUDING

Exploring the necessity of the impossible, having framed the frame, paused over our desire and even faced the impossible, we come to the end. That moment when asking the question is once again leading us back to the initial maze of frustration. But being asked to conclude, do we really remain empty-handed in order for the impossible to exist? Perhaps. Perhaps not.

What is there to conclude, but to continue with the struggle towards life, towards that impossibility that is the only reality that exists after, before, and beyond everything that is? It is the direct consequence of the other; the only possible action for whoever feels trapped by the worldliness of reality. But reality is not philosophy's limit. Facing the limit, facing reality, there is nothing left but to repeat, to retrace our steps that have gotten us here. Rhere is more than the everydayness of the tragic life.

We set up the world as we encounter it, layer by layer we construct and deconstruct it as we live on, minute by minute. We delete and deny, we entertain notions, follow desire. We are trapped in a manner that does not let us stay silent. This is the beginning and the end of creativity — and it is the face behind art. It is what stares right back at us once we remove our own masks, show our hidden being, our being nothing other than the desire to overcome everything that keeps us from experiencing the beyond.

In this age of mechanical reproduction, of digital images that can be repeated incessantly without leaving a mark, in continuous different contexts but increasingly normalising everything, we lose ourselves. We repeat the same, instead of repeating in favour of bringing us back and forward to that moment that breaks time. Instead of feeling the frustration of the impossible, we brainwash ourselves and our surrounding with the sound of the common. We become followers.

We are no longer individuals, but are truly levelled with the commons, the great unwashed. *Hoi polloi.*

And we accept it. *En masse.* Whatever happens, whatever is said, we might protest — but even through, and perhaps precisely because of, our protest, we enjoy the fact that something happens. When we protest, it is from the safety of our *world*, the world that makes everything already understandable, undeniable, decisive from the moment we utter a single world. We protest as long as our world is not in danger. We protest when the bubble we call reality tells us it is time to protest. Even though we are willing to give our lives to face an injustice, to create the world in our own image, we are not willing to question that image. "Moreover it is clear that in the end, despite the intention to reject it, the real world is accepted, since it is transposed, instead of being transformed by knowledge."[394]

Even madness has become a phantasm, a claim for uniqueness that dulls the possible moment of rupture. Even art has become business, the bringing forth of otherness as a simple mechanism to sell and live within a comfortable world. Even love... Well, let's not get into that desire of desire that is abused and taken advantage of precisely because it is what makes us open up towards that which is not already always present: the Other. It is labelled as a vulnerability, a femaleness, a weakness. But even more than art and madness, it is love that can lead us astray in order to forget reality.

394 Henri Lefebvre, *Critique of Everyday Life*, p. 143.

SPEAKING OF THE IMPOSSIBLE

So, in the face of everything we know, what is there to do, what can we write; or is there nothing left to do but to be silent? Is there some kind of writing, acting, being, that embraces the madness of accepting the violence involved in the failure of the continuous desire of becoming human. "Without speech, without another speech except that murmuring voice from an ancient dreadful past."[395] Is there the murmuring of voices that is going on, that will not leave us, that will follow us from the end of time until the end of time, that is the sign of our madness, that is the encroaching of the impossible that becomes present to only be lost again. Is this what becoming human is? Accepting the voices that are present, in life, in writing, in the avoidance of everydayness, in tracing the words that always find themselves hidden in their presence of desiring the other.

I would like to believe there is such a word that tells me of the beyond. But every time I utter it, I am lost once more. Blinded by the desire that urges me to change my whole life, I find myself once again returned to the place I started from. People often ask where you're going to; but, a better question would be to ask *where one is returning to*. That re-turning that is not meant to undo the first turn, but to go back, to relive that one and only decisive moment of one's life: the coming into being, the birth that went by unnoticed, that is celebrated by everyone but you. That moment of taking shape: that is the essence of our desire.

And there is such an uttering that doesn't pose itself as an answer that stupefies, that silences, that makes the impossible impenetrable and leaves all our efforts behind, kills everything without a trace. This uttering is what keeps up from falling, from the annihilation of the impossible.

395 Maurice Blanchot, *Le pas au-delà*, p.33.

This uttering is the question itself. This is the task ahead of us, the task we've been performing and will need to perform. "So this would be for me the great task of thinking today: to redefine and rethink the limits of the possible and the impossible."[396]

396 Slavoj Žižek, *Demanding the Impossible*, p.144.

INCENTIVE

We start out as the progressive children of our time, fighting for whatever we decide upon. The only thing we can wish, as birthdays pass, is to stay true to that desire, the one desire that un-grounds us and our reality. Happiness and dread are equally unimportant when it comes to living, to being human.

There is nothing wrong, morally and socially, with being consumers of the present. Of being followers of the accepted, of the preconditioned revolutions that reinforce the dichotomy that has always already impelled us to accepting reality. The one thing we can start doing, is to accept this reality. To face the fact that this hunger for radical change, this desire that makes us take that step which is a giant leap for mankind, is part of the very same bubble we need not overlook.

Accepting the impossibility as that which remains impossible makes for a different world. It is not relativism that shakes the ground of our being. For all are subsumed under one world, and have turned out to be unshakable in the face of the impossible. By accepting the impossible, we actively refute pessimism and relativism.

It is pessimism that needs to be averted — riding with a dozen armoured knights abreast to face the fact that winter is coming. That winter that is no longer something dooming over the edge, to be kept at bay with illusions of summer. It is this pessimism, this darkness that lies at wait, when we would conclude that there is no change — no radical change. We hole up in our comfortable houses that are the world, that are known to us, but within which we don't even freeze to death. Who is to say that we are alive in the first place?

Perhaps this is why this work is bound to be limited in answering to the original desire for the impossible. For to assert anything — like even pointing at that which cannot be pointed at — would be falling into the same mechanism of desire. We would crush every momentum of possibility that the impossible carries with it, and we would be left at the place where we started. Perhaps it is this eternal recurrence of necessary failure that makes us human.

How is this not pessimism? By acknowledging the hope that lies in trying, by accepting that residing in the present is the only hopelessness. The fact that the Other cannot be reached except through failing to grasp it, is not a reason to stop the effort.

Aiming for the impossible is such an important part of what we call human, that which makes us human. It shakes our very foundation of life, the manner we perceive the world. Instead of relying on the world and surviving, it is our very own existence that is placed in the balance. Puts everything that we know at risk. Yet it also gives everything that we know, and place our trust in, a grounding. Without the beyond, without the presence of the impossible around the corner, life would lose all meaning that we've so desperately tried to attach to it.

Thinking of the beyond, of the impossible, the touch of the other, creates the need for thinking without examples. A thinking that is not limited to the rational, to the epistemic structures that the present presents to us. We need to play, play as a movement against accepting that which comes or doesn't come. "Playing, that is playing against chance and non-chance – that binary logic – in favour of the plurality of the play. But why playing? Yes, playing, even when you're unable to. Playing, that is desiring, desiring without desire, and meanwhile desiring to play."[397]

397 Maurice Blanchot, *Le pas au-delà*, p.43.

CHOOSING OUR OWN SUFFERING

Unwinding the impossible-possible dichotomy while proposing a beyond that is unworldly makes us vulnerable. Not only to relativism and pessimism, but also to the blindness that our own desire provokes. Longing for a solution for any problem, we crush the possibility of the impossible that is not covered by the framing of our issues.

Whether it concerns the finding of the solution leading to world peace, moving beyond the speed of light, or finding a theory of everything – all these questions remain unanswered precisely because we cannot but approach them from the side of the question that is already framed. Our concepts of revolution, change and progress are all biased and make only certain answers possible and therefore make these answers always already insufficient.

The only thing left to do, is to take that leap. "Facing the visible-invisible horizon Greek truth proposes to us (truth as light, light as measure), there is another dimension disclosed to man where, beyond every horizon, he must relate to what is beyond his reach."[398] To radically doubt that frame that has made us into what we are. Risk everything. Risk not getting an answer. Risk having to stop asking the very question that moved us in the first place. Only then, might the real issue underlying all the visible be addressed.

But what about human suffering? When we follow this path, we are no longer looking for answers, we are forgetting questions that have spurred mankind forward for centuries. What about suffering, that basic notion of someone in pain, of unhappiness, of loneliness. Of death.

398 Maurice Blanchot, *The Infinite Conversation*, p.186.

Is it naivety, or can we really say that taking the impossible seriously, putting the notion of the world not in the forefront, accepting the difference and not letting it dictate our very being, is actually a way to move beyond human suffering?

What more insufferable than to be locked in the present? Having the quest of the impossible ahead is more than giving hope to someone. We can have hope by being oblivious to the truth; in the face of death we can hope to live. But when we embrace the impossible, it is not hope that sustains us. Hope is a saying no to possible failure. Embracing the impossible is accepting the failure and at the same time using the failure as a reason to say yes once more.

It is like the story of Sisyphus: the man doomed to roll a big stone up a hill, to only have it fall all the way down when he has almost reached the top. His suffering is extreme. As Heidegger said about Nietzsche's eternal return — the question of how again and again we come to the same point and need to face it — "this 'thought of thoughts' is at the same time 'the most burdensome thought.'"[399] By reaching for the impossible we face the undoing of our world, we lose our identity without getting anything in return, and we know that we need to do it over and over again. The difference with Sisyphus is that we choose this suffering ourselves. But is that what makes this suffering meaningful? Or is this just another lure into the same old ideology-based fascism that keeps our heads up and our feet going somewhere. Somewhere, anywhere – at least not nowhere. Is this supposed to be an uplifting story, is that what everybody is waiting for? The world is the world; there is no way out, keep on trying. If this is what philosophy comes down to, it figures that today's world wants nothing to do with it. The desire to break free leads to the eternal despair of having to undo everything, without method or guideline.

399 Martin Heidegger, *Nietzsche*, p.25.

What moved Sisyphus, what made him go on, day after day, knowing nothing would ever change? Would any hope for a change in his condition make things easier? No. As long as he accepted the world as it was, the comfort of knowing his suffering, of not knowing any other place where such suffering did not exist, he could keep going. If there is something that gives life, it is not the hope that makes us construct worlds beyond our own. True hope lies in the fact that it is us moving within this eternal suffering, the eternal recurrence that is life itself.

Instead of searching for a hope that lies beyond the world we inhabit, we acknowledge the impossibility of breaking the world, of reaching for the Other, that always fails at the same moment that it comes to pass; but that precisely through its failure, comes to pass. This is not hope of breaking away. This is the constitutive moment of the human.

We can we find solace in knowing that this suffering is not brought about by illusion, by consuming the other's frames. Our touching the other can be enough to be new and meaningful, to create a new that is not radical enough to last, but enough to let us repeat it over and over again. The touching that is only possible because of our suffering. Is that what it means when we are summoned as philosophers to ask the question of the human, the impossible, over and over again – to touch that which is untouchable?

BEYOND THE MECHANICS

Is this continuous reaching for the beyond, and the resulting suffering, solving anything? Are the questions that humanity grapples with today now solved by this theory of the world and the impossible?

It might. (If I were to say it does, am I not yet again providing a totalising paradigm that limits that which we want to remain unaware of, that which we want to remain impossible?) What I have done is to describe the mechanics of the possible-impossible and to show the necessity of this continuous desire for the impossible as being an essential human trait. But it is not enough to actually proclaim that the question of how to achieve radical change is now solved. This project is only at the beginning. There are numerous paths to be taken, and they might lead to places that lie beyond any imagining. But all remains unspoken of, unframed, and personal; it is the individual that needs to take up the path that is never before been walked upon. It is the individual that takes up the mirror, and is not afflicted by the illusions of the same and illusions of change that it makes you see: the individual will shatter the mirror and look beyond it. And see nothing, as the seeing of what is-not is already framing, showing, taking care of it; but in this failure there is the beauty that fulfils the desire of the impossible.

The next step in attaining an understanding of radical change in the practical sense could be to see where the touching of the other, of reaching for the beyond the world, can be achieved without limiting the impossible by framing a method. This might prove unattainable; it might not. The probable failure that lies ahead is the reason this project needs to be undertaken. This can be done at a theoretical level, or at a very practical level involving very real issues. Like climate change, war, consumerism.

What is necessary is to find out what the touching of the other means in practical contexts of politics, love, and science. What does it mean to desire the truly other in a political setting without trying to simultaneously frame the other, control it in order to deal with the fear that comes from thinking the impossible? What change to the institutional framework is necessary in order for this reaching for the impossible to be able to happen and to have effect on the manner in which we go about our daily lives, but also on how we make decisions. Both on a personal level and on a communal level. What does it mean to accept failure and continue to repeat the failing approach of the truly other? What does it mean for society if truth and the right decisions are no longer measured according to the episteme that is present in the world, but by the way it turns that episteme around? Would it mean the end of democracy? Or the beginning of a truth-based way of working that truly represents the desire of all peoples?

There is only philosophy. And in the end, the only question that remains and continues to be worth asking for any human being, is the question of the impossible.

That impossible, that beyond which could be labelled God if you will, is, as St. Augustine put it, closer to me than I am to myself.[400] We will remain anxious until we find that, which already is but cannot be seen.

400 "Interior intimo meo" Augustin, *Confessions*, Book III, 6.11.

"We shall not cease from exploration
And the end of all our exploring
Will be to arrive where we started
And know the place for the first time.
Through the unknown, unremembered gate
When the last of earth left to discover
Is that which was the beginning;
At the source of the longest river
The voice of the hidden waterfall
And the children in the apple-tree

Not known, because not looked for
But heard, half-heard, in the stillness
Between two waves of the sea.
Quick now, here, now, always —
A condition of complete simplicity
(Costing not less than everything)
And all shall be well and
All manner of thing shall be well
When the tongues of flames are in-folded
Into the crowned knot of fire
And the fire and the rose are one."

~ T.S. Eliot, *Little Gidding*

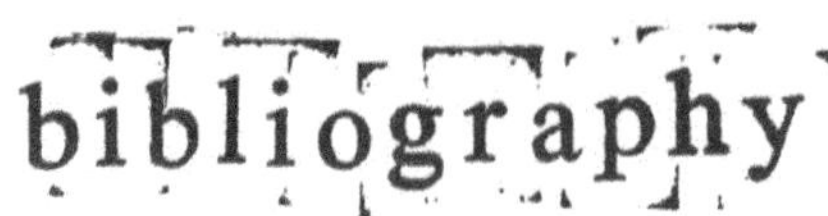

bibliography

- `Abd al-Karīm al-Jīlī, 'On the Sidrat al-Muntahā' in sect. 49 of the *al-Insān al-kāmil* (vol.2 pp.12-13) trans. Stephen Lambden (1997).
- Agamben, Giorgio, *Homo Sacer: Souvereign Power and Bare Life*, Stanford, CA: Stanford University Press 1998.
- Agamben, Giorgio, *Infancy and History: The Destruction of Experience,* New York: Verso Books 1996.
- Agamben, Giorgio, *Remnants of Auschwitz: The Witness and the Archive. Homo Sacer III*, New York: Zone, 2002.
- Agamben, Giorgio, *The Sacrament of Language*, Stanford, CA: Stanford University Press 2011.
- Agamben, Giorgio, *What is an Apparatus?* Stanford, CA: Stanford University Press 2009.
- Arendt, Hannah, *Vita Activa, oder Vom tätigen Leben*, München/Zürich: Piper 2013.
- As-Sa'di, Abd ar-Rahman ibn Nasir, *Taisīr al-karīm al-rahman fī tafsīr kalām al-manān.*
- Augustine, *Confessions,* New York: Image Books 1960.
- Badiou, Alain, *Ethics*, New York: Verso Books 2001.
- Badiou, Alain, *Logics of Worlds*, New York: Continuum 2009.
- Badiou, Alain, *Manifesto for Philosophy*, Albany: SUNY Press 1999.
- Badiou, Alain, *Philosopy for Militants*, New York: Verso Books 2012.

- Badiou, Alain, *Wittgenstein's Antiphilosophy*, New York: Verso Books 2011.
- Barthes, Roland, *Camera Lucida*, New York: Hill and Wang 2010.
- Barthes, Roland, *The Rustle of Language*, New York: Hill and Wang 1987.
- Bataille, Georges, *L'expérience intérieure*, Paris: Gallimard 1973.
- Bataille, Georges, *Méthode de Méditation*, Paris: Gallimard 1973.
- Bataille, Georges, *Unfinished System of Nonknowledge*, Minneapolis: University of Minneapolis Press 2001.
- Bataille, Georges, *Visions of Excess*, Minneapolis: University of Minnesota Press 1985.
- Benjamin, Walter, *Early Writings*, Cambridge: The Belknap Press of Harvard University Press 2011.
- Benjamin, Walter, *Gesammelte Schriften II*, Frankfurt am Main: Suhrkamp Verlag 1974.
- Benjamin, Walter, *Illuminations*, New York: Schocken Books 1969.
- Benjamin, Walter, *Reflections: Essays, Aphorisms, Autobiographical Writings*, New York: Random House USA Inc 1995.
- Berlinski, David, *A Tour of the Calculus*, New York: Pantheon Books 1995.
- Blanchot, Maurice, *L'autreamont et Sade*, Paris: Editions de Minuit 1949.
- Blanchot, Maurice, *The Gaze of Orpheus*, New York: Station Hill 1981.

- Blanchot, Maurice, *The Infinite Conversation*, Minneapolis: University of Minneapolis Press 1993.
- Blanchot, Maurice, *The Space of Literature*, Lincoln: University of Nebraska Press 1989.
- Blanchot, Maurice, *The Step Not Beyond*, New York: State University of New York Press, 1992.
- Blanchot, Maurice, *The Unavowable Community*, Barrytown: Station Hill Press 1985.
- Blanchot, Maurice, *Works of Fire*, Stanford: Stanford University Press 1981.
- Borges, Jorges Luis, *A Personal Anthology*, New York: Grove Press 1994.
- Butler, Judith, *Bodies that Matter*, London: Routledge 2011.
- Butler, Judith, *Excitable Speech : A Politics of the Performative*, New York: Routledge, 1997.
- Cioran, Emil, *On the Heights of Madness*, Chicago: University of Chicago Press 1992.
- Deleuze, Gilles, *Desire and Pleasure*, In: Magazine littéraire 325, October 1994, pp. 59-65.
- Deleuze, Gilles, *Difference and Repetition*, New York: Columbia University Press 1995.
- Deleuze, Gilles, *Negotiations*, New York: Columbia University Press 1995.
- Deleuze, Gilles, *Woran erkennt man den Strukturalismus?* Berlin: Merve Verlag 1992.
- Deleuze, Gilles and Félix Guattari, *A Thousand Plateus*, Minneapolis: Minnesota University Press 1987.

- Deleuze, Gilles and Félix Guattari, *Qu'est-ce que la philosophie?* Paris: Minuit 1991.
- De Man, Paul, *Allegories on Reading*, New Haven: Yale University Press 1979.
- De Man, Paul, *"Conclusions" on Walter Benjamin's "The Task of the Translator" Messenger Lecture, Cornell University, March 4, 1983*, Yale French Studies 69, 1985.
- Democritus, *Ancilla to the Pre-Socratic Philosophers: A Complete Translation of the Fragments in Diels*, Cambridge MA: Harvard University Press 1948.
- Derrida, Jacques, *A Certain Impossible Possibility of Saying the Event*, Critical Inquiry, Vol. 33, No. 2, pp. 441-461.
- Derrida, Jacques, *Aporias*, Stanford: Standford University Press 1993.
- Derrida, Jacques, "Autoimmunity: Real and Symbolic Suicides" and "Deconstructing Terrorism," In: Giovanna Borradori, *Philosophy in a Time of Terror: Dialogues with Jürgen Habermas and Jacques Derrida*, Chicago: University of Chicago Press 2003.
- Derrida, Jacques, "Cogito et histoire de la folie" In: *L'Ecriture et la différence*, Paris: Le Seuil 1967.
- Derrida, Jacques, *Marges de la philosophie*, Paris: Minuit 1967.
- Derrida, Jacques, *Papier Machine*, Stanford: Stanford University Press 2005.
- Derrida, Jacques, *Positions*, Chicago: University of Chicago Press
- Derrida, Jacques, *Voyous,* Paris: Galilée 2003.
- Derrida, Jacques and Anne Dufourmantelle, *Of Hospitality*, Stanford: Stanford University Press 2000.

- Dufourmantelle, Anne, *Accueillir l'inespéré*, http://www.lutecium.org/convergencia/convergencia_files/Anne%20Dufourmantelle.pdf, [June 2019]
- Eagleton, Terry, *Figures of Dissent*, London: Verso 2003.
- Elliot, T.S., *Four Quartets*, San Diego: Harcourt 1943.
- Felman, Shoshana, *Writing and Madness,* Palo Alto: Stanford University Press 2003.
- Feltham, Oliver, *Alain Badiou: Live Theory*, London: Bloomsbury Academic 2008.
- Fernando, Jeremy, *Reading Blindly*, New York: Cambria Press 2009.
- Fink, Bruce, *The Lacanian Subject: Between Language and Jouissance,* Princeton: Princeton University Press 1996.
- Foucault, Michel, *Abnormal*, London: Picador 2004.
- Foucault, Michel, *Discipline and Punish*, New York: Random House 1975.
- Foucault, Michel, *Histoire de la folie à l'âge classique*, Paris: Gallimard 1972.
- Foucault, Michel, *Power/Knowledge: Selected Interviews and Other Writing, 1972-1977*, New York: Pantheon Books 1980.
- Foucault, Michel, *The Archaeology of Knowledge*, London: Routledge 2002.
- Foucault, Michel, *The Order of Things,* London: Routledge 2004.
- Fynsk, Christopher, *Language & Relation*, Stanford: Stanford University Press 1996.
- Fynsk, Christopher, *Last Steps: Maurice Blanchot's exilic writing*, New York: Fordham University Press 2013.

- Gadamer, Hans-Georg, *The Relevance of the Beautiful*, Cambridge: Cambridge University Press 1998.
- Gadamer, Hans-Georg, *Philosophical Hermeneutics*, Berkeley: University of California Press 1976.
- Goodman, Nelson, *Ways of Worldmaking*, Indianapolis: Hackett 1978.
- Hand, Séan, *Emmanuel Levinas*, London: Routledge 2009.
- Harman, Graham, *The Quadruple Object*, Winchester: Zero Books 2011.
- Hegel, Georg Wilhelm Friedrich, *Encyklopädie der philosophischen Wissenschaften im Grundrisse*, Vol. 1: *Die Logik*, Berlin: Dunder and Humboldt 1843.
- Heidegger, Martin, *Holzwege*, Gesamtausgabe 5, Frankfürt am Main: Vittorio Klostermann 2003.
- Heidegger, Martin, *Introduction to Metaphysics*, Yale: Yale University Press 2000.
- Heidegger, Martin, "Letter on Humanism", In: D. F. Krell (ed.), *Basic Writings*, London: Routledge 1978.
- Heidegger, Martin, *Logik*, Gesamtausgabe 21, Frankfürt am Main: Vittorio Klostermann 1976.
- Heidegger, Martin, *Poetry, Language, Thought*, New York: HarperCollins 2001.
- Heidegger, Martin, *Sein und Zeit*, Gesamtausgabe 2, Frankfürt am Main: Vittorio Klostermann 1977.
- Heidegger, Martin, *The Eternal Recurrence of the Same* (trans. David Farrell Krell.) New York: Harper and Row 1984.
- Heidegger, Martin, *The Origin of the Work of Art*, In: *Basic Writings*, New York: HarperCollins 2008.

- Heidegger, Martin, *The Question Concerning Technology and Other Essays*, New York: Garland Publishing, 1977.
- Heidegger, Martin, *Unterwegs zur Sprache*, Gesamtausgabe 12, Frankfürt am Main: Vittorio Klostermann 1985.
- Heidegger, Martin, *Vorträge und Aufsätze,* Gesamtausgabe 7, Frankfürt am Main: Vittorio Klostermann 2000.
- Heidegger, Martin, *What is Called Thinking?* New York: Harper & Row 1968.
- Heraclitus, *Homeric Questions*, in: Franz Oelmann, *Heracliti Quaestiones homericae / ediderunt societatis philologae bonnensis sodales.* Leipzig: Teubner 1910.
- Husserl, Edmund, *Cartesian Meditations: An Introduction to Pure Phenomenology*, Dordrecht: Martinus Nijhoff 1988.
- Kant, Immanuel, *An Answer to the Question: What is Enlightenment*, In: *Practical Philosophy*, Cambridge: Cambridge University Press 1996.
- Kant, Immanuel, "The Conflict of Faculties", in: *Political Writings*, Cambridge: Cambridge University Press 1991.
- Kant, Immanuel, *Kritik der reinen Vernunft*, Frankfürt am Main: Suhrkamp 1974.
- Karlberg, Michael, *Beyond the Culture of Contest*, Oxford: Georg Ronald 2004.
- Kierkegaard, Soren, *Sickness unto Death*, Princeton: Princeton University Press 1983.
- Kofman, Sarah, "Beyond Aporia?" In: Benjamin, Andrew, *Post-Structuralist Classics,* London: Routledge 1983.
- Kuhn, Thomas, *The Essential Tension*, Chicago: University of Chicago Press 1977.

- Lacan, Jacques, *Ecrits*, New York: W. W. Norton & Company 1977.
- Lacan, Jacques, *The Seminar of Jacques Lacan: Book I: Freud's Papers on Technique 1953–1954*, New York: W. W. Norton & Company 1991.
- Laclau, Ernesto and Mouffe, Chantal, *Hegemony and Social Strategy*, London: Verso Books 1985.
- Lampden, Stephen http://www.hurqalya.pwp.blueyonder.co.uk/baha'i%20encyclopedia/SID-RAH-SIDRAT-BE.htm [July 2014]
- Lao Tzu, *Tao Te Ching*, Tokyo: Kodansha International 2010.
- Lathouwers, Ton, *Zen Talks*, Amsterdam: Vrije Universiteit Press 2013.
- Lawlor, Leonard, *Thinking through French Philosophy*, *The Being of the Question*, Indiana: Indiana University Press 2003.
- Lefebvre, Henri, *Critique of Everyday Life*, London: Verso Books 2014.
- Levinas, Emmanuel, *"Is Ontology Fundamental?"* (1951), in: *Entres Nous. On Thinking-of-the-Other*, London: Athlone Press 1998.
- Levinas, Emmanuel, *Nine Talmudic Readings*, Indianapolis: Indiana University Press 1990.
- Levinas, Emmanuel, *Sur Maurice Blanchot*, Montpellier: Fata Morgana 1975.
- Levinas, Emmanuel, *The Trace of the Other*, In: *Deconstruction in Context*, Chicago: University of Chicago Press, 1986.
- Levinas, Emmanuel, *Totality and Infinity*, Pittsburgh: Duquesne University Press 1969.

- Lloyd, Genevieve, *The Man of Reason: "Male" and "Female" in Western Philosophy*, London: Routledge 1995.
- Lyotard, Jean-François, *The Inhuman: Reflections on Time,* Stanford University Press 1991.
- Lyotard, Jean-François, *Re-Writing Modernity,* SubStance Vol. 16, No. 3, Issue 54 (1987), pp. 3-9.
- MacIntyre, Alasdair, *Three Rival Versions of Moral Enquiry*, Notre Dame University Press 1990.
- Markson, David, *Wittgenstein's Misstress,* Champaign, Ill: Dalkey Archive Press 1988.
- Meillassoux, Quentin, *After Finitude,* London: Bloomsbury Academic 2010.
- Meillassoux, Quentin, "Potentiality and Virtuality", in: *Collapse: Philosophical Research and Development*, 2, 2007.
- Merleau-Ponty, Maurice, *Phenomenology of Perception,* London: Routledge 2004.
- Mills, Sara, *Discourse*, London: Routledge 1997.
- Nancy, Jean-Luc, *The being-with of being-there,* in: Continental Philosophical Review (2008), 41.
- Nietzsche, Friedrich, *Beyond Good and Evil,* London: Penguin 2003.
- Nietzsche, Friedrich, *Ecce Homo*, London: Penguin 2005.
- Nietzsche, Friedrich, *Jenseits von Gut und Böse – Zur Geneologie der Moral*, München: De Gruyter 1999.
- Nietzsche, Friedrich, *Götzen-Dämmerung*, KGW 6.3, Berlin: Walter de Gruyter Verlag 2001.

- Plato, *Meno and Other Dialogues*, Oxford: Oxford University Press 2005.
- Plato, *Republic*, New York: Basic Books 1991.
- Puntel, Lorenz, *Struktur und Sein*, Tübingen: Mohr Siebeck Verlag 2006.
- Raffould, François, *The Origins of Responsibility*, Bloomington: Indiana University Press 2010.
- Rescher, Nicholas, *Aporetics*, Pittsburgh: University of Pittsburgh Press 2009.
- Ricoeur, Paul, *Text to Action*, Evanston: Northwestern University Press 1991.
- Ricoeur, Paul, *The Reality of the Historical Past*, Milwaukee: Marquette University Press, 1984.
- Rückert, Friedrich, *Deutsche Balladen*, Stuttgart: Philipp Reclam 1995.
- Sartre, Jean-Paul, *Being and Nothingness*, London: Routledge 2003.
- Schiller, Friedrich, *Thalia*, Erster Band 2, Leipzig: Georg Joachim Göschen Verlag 1785.
- Schirmacher, Wolfgang, *Technik und Gelassenheit. Zeitkritik nach Heidegger*. Fermenta philosophica, München: Alber Freiburg 1983.
- Shepherdson, Charles, *Lacan and the Limits of Language*, New York: Fordham University Press 2008.
- Spencer, Herbert, *First Principles*, Cambridge: Cambridge University Press 2009.

- Valéry, Paul, *Aesthetics*, New York: Pantheon Books 1964.
- Walzer, Michael, *Spheres of Justice: A Defense of Pluralism and Equality*, Basic Books 1983.
- Weil, Simone, *Draft for a Statement of Human Obligation*, http://www.pbs.org/wgbh/questionof-god/voices/weil.html [August 2014].
- Weil, Simone, *Grace and Gravity*, New York & London: Routledge 2003.
- Wittgenstein, Ludwig, *Philosophical Investigations*, Upper Saddle River: Prentice Hall 1999.
- Wittgenstein, Ludwig, *Tractatus logico-philosophicus*, London: Routledge 2001.
- Yoran, Gabriel, *The Interfact*, Dissertation European Graduate School 2017.
- Young, Julian, *Heidegger's Philosophy of Art*, Cambridge: Cambridge University Press 2001.
- Žižek, Slavoj, *Demanding the Impossible*, Cambridge: Polity 2013.
- Žižek, Slavoj, *How To Read Lacan*, New York: W. W. Norton & Company 2007.
- Žižek, Slavoj, *Less than Nothing*, London: Verso Books 2013.
- Žižek, Slavoj, *On Alain Badiou and Logiques des mondes*, http://www.lacan.com/zizbadman.htm [April 2014].
- Žižek, Slavoj, *Organs without Bodies*, London: Routledge 2003.

www.ingramcontent.com/pod-product-compliance
Ingram Content Group UK Ltd.
Pitfield, Milton Keynes, MK11 3LW, UK
UKHW021650190726
13853UKWH00001B/178

9 789083 016405